WHAT HOLLYWOOD IS SAYING ABOUT
NEXT! AN ACTOR'S GUIDE TO AUDITIONING . . .

Steve Oedekerk, actor/ comedian, also writer and director of *Ace Ventura 2: When Nature Calls* says: "Loved **NEXT!** A much-needed text. Finally actors can peek over to the other side of the Great Auditioning Wall. Being comfortable with the auditioning process is perhaps one of the hardest things to master in the world of acting. **NEXT!** supplies the tools to achieve that goal . . . . ALL ACTORS READ **NEXT!** If actors can change their perception of the audition process from an obstacle to that of a positive opportunity, it will indeed change careers. Congratulations to Ellie [Kanner] and Paul [Bens] for taking the mystery and tension out of a very mysteriously tense process."

K Callan, Actress/Author *Lois & Clark: The New Adventures of Superman* says: "Ellie Kanner and Paul Bens have written the definitive auditioning guide for actors. They not only tell you why you're not getting the auditions, they tell you how to get an audition, how to behave at an audition, and how to negotiate once you get the job. There's even a sample deal memo. Besides all the inside audition information, they tell you how the casting director has to audition for his job. ACTORS, YOU GOTTA HAVE THIS BOOK!"

Rudy Hornish, Vice President, Grammnet Productions, says: "As an actor-turned-producer, I highly recommend **NEXT!** as required reading for everyone involved in the casting process. This book not only provides actors with all they need to know about auditioning, it could also be quite enlightening for producers, writers, and directors as well."

MORE PRAISE FOR
NEXT! AN ACTOR'S GUIDE TO AUDITIONING . . .

James Burrows, director of Cheers, Friends, Taxi, etc., says: "Ellie Kanner is a casting director with terrific ability, as shown by her faith in the young "Friends" cast. This book serves as a primer for all actors. It will guide you, educate you, and teach you the ins and outs of what a casting director is looking for. It will give you everything but the talent. That you have to be born with."

Lori Openden, Senior Vice President, Talent and Casting, NBC Entertainment, says: "One of the most misunderstood aspects of casting is that we are not rooting for the actor. The truth is, we support the actors who audition for us. Perhaps knowing that we are behind them 100 percent will give them the confidence they need to do their best on an audition."

Deborah Joy LeVine, creator of Lois & Clark: The New Adventures of Superman says: "Ellie [Kanner] cast two of my television series: Lois & Clark: The New Adventures of Superman and Courthouse. Believe me, in those weekly casting sessions, we've seen it all. It constantly amazes me how so many working actors know so little about the audition process. If only they would pick up a copy of **NEXT!** and study it, they would stand a much better chance of landing the job. Ellie [Kanner] and Paul [Bens]'s book should be mandatory reading for any actor smart enough to realize that it all starts with the audition, and can easily end there as well."

NEXT!

An Actor's Guide to Auditioning

Ellie Kanner, C. S. A., and Paul G. Bens, Jr.

lone eagle

NEXT! An Actors Guide to Auditioning
Copyright © 1997 by Ellie Kanner and Paul G. Bens, Jr.

LONE EAGLE PUBLISHING CO.™
1024 North Orange Drive
Hollywood, California 90038
Tel 323.308.3400 or 800.FILMBKS
A division of IFILM℠ Corp., www.ifilm.com

Printed in the United States of America
Cover design by Heidi Frieder
10 9 8 7 6 5 4 3

Library of Congress Cataloging in Publication Data

Kanner, Ellie
Next! : an actor's guide to auditioning / Ellie Kanner and Paul G. Bens, Jr.
p. cm.
Includes bibliographical references and index.
ISBN: 0-943728-71-1 (pbk.)
1. Acting—Auditions. I. Bens, Paul G., Jr.
PN2071.A92K36 1996
792'.028—dc20   96-46181
                                                         CIP

Lone Eagle books may be purchased in bulk at special discounts for promotional or educational purposes. Special editions can be created to specifications. Inquiries for sales and distribution, textbook adoption, foreign language translation, editorial, and rights and permissions inquiries should be addressed to: Jeff Black, Lone Eagle Publishing, 1024 North Orange Drive, Hollywood, California 90038 or send e-mail to: info@loneeagle.com

Distributed to the trade by National Book Network, 800.462.6420

Lone Eagle Publishing Company™ is a registered trademark.
IFILM℠ is a registered service mark.

FOREWORD

by MATT LeBLANC

So you wanna know more about auditions. Well, you'll have good and bad ones. That's a guarantee. Ones you think went well, didn't. Others where you think you tanked, you shined. All in all, you never know what the powers that be (director, producer, etc.) are looking for. Sure, your agent, manager or the list in Breakdown will give you a rough sketch of the role, but it's up to the actor to take the sketch, add the color and pull it off the page.

Often your only ally in the audition-situation is the casting director. The casting director is the liaison between you and the aforementioned powers that be. They know what they want. A few key words of advice on your way into the room can inspire confidence, give you insight and help you tweak your adaptation of the role—enough so that, hopefully, you will be successful in keeping your rent paid.

Preparation is key to an actor's job. Often, however, there is little or no time to prepare. Thus the importance to the actor of the casting director.

Ellie Kanner is the type of casting director I speak of. She's sensitive, creative, kind and supportive. Now that Ellie and Paul have written this book, I can't tell you how lucky you are to have at your disposal their words of wisdom. This book will steer you through open-calls, pre-reads, callbacks and second callbacks. It'll take you through the right questions to ask and how to limit distractions at the audition. It gives you post audition advice like how to put together a successful team and negotiate a deal.

If you are wise, you'll follow their advice and obtain answers. If not, be prepared to ask a lot of questions like—"Do you want fries with that?"

Good luck with your career.

Matt LeBlanc

P.S. Hey, Ellie, thanks again for the callback on *Friends*.

INTRODUCTION

As an actor, how do you feel about casting directors? Many actors tend to look upon us as foes in the battle for employment, seeing us as an obstacle. We're the decision-maker. We're to be feared.

In actuality, we are not your enemy. We're your compatriots.

We realize that the antagonistic relationship which seems to exist between *casting directors* and actors may be difficult to shake, but that is one of the reasons we wanted to write this book. As casting directors, we want to help dispel the myths and alleviate any trepidation you may have when meeting us, in addition to sharing many of the "tricks of the trade." We want to fill you in on whom we are, what we do and what we can do for you.

As you read through the following pages, you will notice that we have italicized certain words or phrases which are important terms for every actor to know. While seasoned professionals may be familiar with these, newcomers to the industry will find a glossary of these terms in the reference section of this book.

WHOM WE ARE

As with any profession, casting directors come from all different backgrounds and different parts of the country. They have one thing in common—they are simply trying to do their jobs the best they can. Casting directors have parents, husbands, wives, lovers,

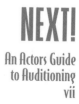

children, car problems, financial woes, and job problems just as you may have. They have good days and bad days, feelings and emotions, stress and relief, dreams and expectations.

Like some of you, many casting directors came into this industry wanting to do something else. Paul, for example, came to Los Angeles after having trained extensively as an actor. After two years of going from audition to audition and landing small parts here and there (with quick eyes you might be able to spy Paul in a repeat of a NEW TWILIGHT ZONE episode), he actually landed in casting thanks to friend and casting director, April Webster.

Over dinner one evening, April discussed the *low-budget feature*, Adventure at Spirit Island, she was casting and how frustrating it was that the production had not provided her with a casting assistant. Thinking it would be an incredible learning experience to see exactly what happens on the other side of the casting desk, Paul offered to help.

After that job was completed, Paul went back to acting but jumped quickly at the chance to work with Webster again on . One thing lead to another, and April asked Paul to work for her full-time as her assistant on NBC's NIGHT COURT. It was an agonizing decision to leave acting (food or starvation were the deciding factors), but Paul opted for the stability of a full-time job. He's been in casting ever since.

Ellie had done some acting in college and, when she came to Los Angeles, was not clear that embarking upon an acting career was exactly what she wanted to do. She knew, however, that whatever she ended up doing in the entertainment industry, learning the business end was an absolute necessity.

Like many aspiring new arrivals in L.A., Ellie headed straight to Samuel French bookstore to begin her research. In the industry reference section she found a guide book, opened it, and found a detailed listing of talent agencies in the area. She went down the list one-by-one, calling each agency to see if they were looking to hire a receptionist or assistant. Before even having to go to the second page of agents' names, Ellie struck gold. An agency handling

some of Los Angeles' hottest stand-up comedians, offered Ellie a job as an assistant. A year and a half later, she was given the opportunity to create and head a film and television division for the agency.

While working at the agency, a friend phoned to ask Ellie if she would be interested in casting a play and, eager to learn another side of the industry, she jumped at the opportunity, finding the work challenging but very enjoyable. Shortly after, another friend asked her to cast a *short film* he was directing, and she was hooked.

By this time, Ellie had met Paul Bens and asked him (as well as many others) how she would go about getting into casting on a full-time basis. Paul laid out the huge pay cut she would have to take, threw unemployment statistics at her, and generally tried to dissuade her from taking the risk of moving into an oversaturated job market.

Ellie left the talent agency and landed at Champion/Basker Casting. She began to work on *feature films, series, pilots* and *movies-of-the-week (MOWs)*. In 1990 she moved to Lorimar/Warner Bros., and by 1991 was promoted by Barbara Miller to the position of casting director.

Both of us faced major decisions, wondering all the time if it was the right thing to do. Some days we still wonder . . . .

ACKNOWLEDGMENTS

Thank you to all the actors who have auditioned for me over the years. You make my work exciting and challenging. If you learn one thing from this book that will help you with the auditioning process, I will be deeply satisfied.

To everyone who has given me the opportunity to work for them—especially Irvin Arthur, Deborah Joy LeVine, Barbara Miller, and Helen Mossler—I am deeply indebted to you all.

To Paul Bens for agreeing to write this book with me, thanks for putting up with the late rewrite nights during pilot season and for your friendship over the years. Thanks to everyone at Lone Eagle Publishing, especially Bethann Wetzel, for her many hours of hard work, advice and encouragement, and Joan Singleton for her support and guidance throughout the publishing process.

Many thanks to Matt LeBlanc for writing the foreword, always being so sweet and supportive and for taking me skydiving.

A number of talented colleagues and friends, many of whom are both, gave me advice and quotes during the writing of this book. They all deserve top billing, on a separate card, above title. Since that's not possible, I'll list them alphabetically. They are:

Dean Cain, K Callan, Twink Caplan, Victor Fresco, Jessica Hecht, Rudy Hornish, Ted Hann, Scott Howard, Ken Iwamasa, Lorna Johnson, Sharon Lawrence, Geraldine Leder, John Levey, Leslie Litt, Steve Oedekerk, Lori Openden, Leah Remini, Mark Saks, Debbie Savitt, Anthony Sepulveda, Arleen Sorkin, Eric Stoltz, and Dori Zuckerman. You all have my heartfelt thanks and appreciation.

A special thanks to my parents, Sid and Shirley, and my sister, Susan, for telling me my whole life that I could accomplish anything.

Most of all, thanks to my partner in life, best friend and husband, David, for his love, support and notes!—E. K.

There are many individuals to thank, for without them, not only would **NEXT!** have been impossible to complete, but my personal and professional lives would have truly crumbled.

Most importantly, my thanks goes out to those closest to my heart, though furthest from my location . . . my family: Paul and Judith Bens (miss you, Mom); Mary Beth, Jon, Jonathan and Nathan Oser; Leslie, Randy and Morgan Peterson; and Mary Lou, Ellis, James and Corina Cromer.

For teaching me about acting, my sincere gratitude to Dr. Ron Mielech of Thomas More College. For teaching me about actors and for giving me a true career, my love to April Webster for that and her friendship, too. For their guidance and faith in Melton/Bens Casting, Bob Harbin, Bob Huber and Wendi Matthews of FBC deserve so much more than flowers. For all the gifts given to Pat and me by Columbia/TriStar, we are indebted to Jon Feltheimer, Andy Kaplan, Eric Tannenbaum, Russ Krasnoff, Helene Michaels, Jeanie Bradley, Jocelyn Freid, Kim Haswell, Carl Beverly, Joanne Mazzu, Clay Lorinsky, and Nick Grad. To superagent Mark Scroggs, thanks for the friendship, laughs, and negotiating skills.

Finally, my thanks to Ellie Kanner for asking me to coauthor **NEXT!**; to Joan Singleton and Bethann Wetzel of Lone Eagle Publishing for believing in it; to all those who read, reread, and gave us notes on this monster; and to the best partner a casting director could ask for, Pat Melton. who put up with my fatigued whining while Ellie and I wrote it. Most of all, I dedicate this book to the best actor I know, Jusak Yang Bernhard, whose spirit and photograph should appear in the dictionary simultaneously next to the words, "supportive" and "friend."—P. B.

CONTENTS

FOREWORD by Matt LeBlanc v

INTRODUCTION vii

ACKNOWLEDGMENTS xi

1   CASTING DIRECTORS DEFINED 1
     What Casting Directors Do 1
     What Casting Directors Can Do For You 5

2   BEFORE THE AUDITION 7
     Headshots 7
     Resumes 14
     Demo Reels 17

3   THE CASTING TEAM 23
     Casting Intern 23
     Reader 23
     Casting Assistant 24
     Casting Associate 24
     Casting Director 25

4   TYPES OF AUDITIONS 27
     Cattle Call 27
     Preread 29
     Callback 29
     Screen Test 34
     Network Test 34

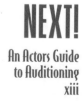

5   GETTING YOUR FOOT IN THE DOOR **43**
    Agent/Manager Submission 43
    Submitting Yourself 44
    Audition Crashing 46

6   QUESTIONS TO ASK ABOUT THE AUDITION **47**
    For Whom Are You Auditioning? 47
    What Materials You Need 48
    When Should You Be There? 51
    Where Are you Going? 52
    Why You should Ask Questions 52

7   IN THE CASTING OFFICE **57**
    Watch Your Words 57
    Psyching Out the Competition 58
    Silence Is Golden 59
    Cleanliness is Next to Godliness 59
    Have Everything You Need 59
    Use Your Common Sense 60

8   IN THE AUDITION **63**
    Letting Go Of Stress 63
    First Impressions 64
    Getting Physical 65
    Saying The Wrong Thing 67
    The Art of Conversation 69
    Props 71
    Changing The Dialogue 71
    Countering Distraction 72
    Getting and Taking Direction 73
    Instant Callbacks 75
    Troubleshooting 76

9   AND THE JOB GOES TO **85**
    Physical Type 85
    Star Power 86
    Friends & Family 86
    Your Own Worst Enemy 86
    Competition 87

10 NEGOTIATING THE DEAL **89**

NEXT!
An Actors Guide
to Auditioning

11   WORKING **101**
   What is expected of you 101
   On-Set Behavior 102
   Being Replaced 103

12   "AND I'D LIKE TO THANK . . . " **105**
   Thank You Notes 105
   Postcards 105
   Photograph and Resume Mailings 106
   Videotapes 107
   Faxes 107
   Phone Calls 107
   Dropping By 108

13   YOUR TEAM AND HOW TO FIND THEM **109**
   Talent Agents 109
   Managers 109
   Publicists 111

REFERENCE SECTION **115**
   Unions & Guilds 115
   Suggested Reading 117
   Networks, Cable and Production Companies 125
   Major Studios 129

GLOSSARY **131**

INDEX **157**

ABOUT THE AUTHORS **162**

INDEX OF ILLUSTRATIONS
   Script Breadown Page 4
   Head Shot—Man 12
   Head Shot—Woman 13
   Bad Resume 18
   Good Resume 19
   Test Option Deal 38
   Audition Checklist 55
   Sample Submission Letter 45
   Casting Deal Memo 90

NEXT!
An Actors Guide
to Auditioning

CASTING DIRECTORS DEFINED

Ever wondered how a casting director gets a job? Like actors, they also have to *audition* but in a completely different way. The casting director's audition is based on their knowledge of the available talent pool, their relationship with talent agents and managers, as well as on their creative vision of each character in the project.

Before meeting on a project, a casting director reads the script and begins to form ideas as to which actors would be best for the piece. He presents these thoughts to the producers, hoping all the while that the producers will be impressed and want to hire him for the job. Whether the producers do or not depends upon how everyone's personalities mesh, their mutual taste and style, as well as experience.

Competition is tough, especially in Los Angeles where there are over four hundred active casting directors. Most wait for the phone to ring, face rejection (sometimes gracefully and sometimes not), and wish for the day when projects are simply offered to them. Sound familiar?

WHAT CASTING DIRECTORS DO

Contrary to popular belief, casting directors are usually not in the position to decide which actor is hired. They do a very specific job— present *producers* with choices.

Casting directors save the producer time by sifting through the available talent pool, choosing the actors best suited for a specific role, and introducing those actors to the producers and director through the audition process. This way, the producers can concentrate on the myriad of other decisions they have to make on a daily basis. While casting directors often have input into whom is hired, the ultimate decision is always made by the producers and the director.

Once a casting director is hired for a specific job, they reread the script and begin to form an image of each character in their mind's eye. Here is where the creative side of casting begins and the process is nearly the same for every casting office.

Lists

Immediately after reading the script, a casting director will jot down the names of actors they feel are right for a particular role. These lists are usually divided into two different types, name-value lists and actor lists.

A *name-value list* is usually compiled when the producers, *studio executives* or *network executives* are intent upon their project having a star in one of the lead roles, or if they want to *stunt cast* (the television term used when executives want to boost the *ratings* by hiring an established star for one of the *guest starring* roles). Once a name-value list is completed, it is sent to the producers so that they may choose the actors they are interested in.

An *actor list* is compiled on every project and is a catalogue of the casting director's first choices for each role. This list will include actors with whom the casting director has worked in the past, actors they would like to work with, and those whose work the casting director is familiar with but has never met. Chances are your name will fall on this list if the casting director knows and likes your work.

Availabilities

Once a casting director completes the lists, he will begin to check *availabilities* on all of those actors. Checking availabilities consists of calling each artist's representatives and asking a series of questions:

1. Is the actor available to work on the dates the character is scheduled to *shoot?* If not, what project are they (will they) be working on and until what date? Is that conflicting project shooting in or out of town?

2. Will the actor work for the amount of money budgeted? If not, what is the minimum amount they will work for?

3. Will the actor audition for the casting director? If not, will they audition for the producers?

4. If the actor is not available to audition but is available for the job, will the actor either go on tape or send a demo tape?

5. If an actor will not read for either the casting director or producer, are they willing to do this particular type of project (i.e., television series, guest star, *cameo*)? If so, notations are made that this actor will work for an *offer only.*

Breakdowns

When the lists have been completed and availabilities have been checked, a casting director will know if it is necessary to meet additional actors for each role. If the casting director needs, wants, or has the time to meet actors new to him or her (or if he simply wants to see who *is* available for the project) he will release a *breakdown* to all talent representatives.

A breakdown, released to agents exclusively through the Breakdown Services, Ltd., is essentially a request for agents to submit actors they feel are appropriate for each particular role. A typical breakdown will include the name of the project, the *network, production company* or studio involved; the names of the producers, writers, *director,* casting director, *casting associate,* and *casting assistant;* a detailed plot summary, work dates, and *location;*

NEXT!
An Actors Guide
to Auditioning

(File 0410p02-rh) L
(Original 0208p-3-lk) L

PARAMOUNT
"FIRED"
1/2 HOUR/NBC
DRAFT: 1/9/96

Executive Producers: Victor Fresco/Kelsey Grammer/ Rudy Hornish
Co-executive Producers: Arleen Sorkin/Paul Slansky
Director: James Burrows
Writers: Victor Fresco, Arleen Sorkin, Paul Slansky
Casting Director: Ellie Kanner
Casting Associate: Debbie Savitt
Start Date: Tentatively, May 28, 1996
Location: Los Angeles

WRITTEN SUBMISSIONS ONLY TO:

ELLIE KANNER
PARAMOUNT STUDIOS
5555 MELROSE AVENUE
SWANSON BUILDING 101
LOS ANGELES, CA 90038

DANNY: A handsome young man in his **EARLY 20s,** Danny is Terry's more fun-loving brother. He's a positive guy with an up attitude, a natural flirt. Danny has his hand in many things. If you need anything, Danny is someone who always knows a guy who knows a guy who can get it for you. He's not above bending the rules, but at his core, he's a good person. Danny, who works as a bartender at the bar and grill downstairs, has always wanted to be a screenwriter, and occasionally he writes articles for a local one-sheet newspaper. Because he likes to have fun, he has a hard time focusing on any one thing for very log. When the fun goes out of it, it's time to move on. Danny thinks that life's too short to keep doing something you don't enjoy doing . . . . SERIES REGULAR. [Copyright 1996, Breakdown Services, Ltd.]

GUY: **LATE 40S TO EARLY 50S,** divorced . . . debonair with a touch of sleaziness . . . he's been in the nightclub business for 20 years and may or may not be "connected." He was a very handsome young man, and has lived and played hard. When he looks in the mirror, he still seems himself at 25, and has the ambition and libido of someone who thinks he's going to live forever. Life's rules don't apply to him (e.g., smoking gives other people cancer) . . . RECURRING. [Copyright 1996, Breakdown Services, Ltd.]

STORY LINE: When the efficient, perfectionist, TERRY, is fired from her job as an assistant to GWEN, she is depressed, but decides to use her nest egg to buy a little time before she starts working again, possibly as her own boss. Gwen, on the other hand, is a brilliant thinker used to living on "an 80s salary too far into the 90s.") When she's fired, she has a lot of trouble landing on her feet, and eventually winds up asking Terry, in her own inimitable style, if she can live with her. Despite their affectionate but chronic personal friction, both Terry and Gwen acknowledge how well their partnership worked—and decided to go into business together . . .

Sample Breakdown page from Breakdown Services, Ltd.

NEXT!
An Actors Guide
to Auditioning

submission address, the size of the role (i.e., *lead, guest star*), and an in-depth character description of each role available.

Breakdowns are delivered to subscribing talent agencies and *personal managers* five days a week (Monday through Friday) in several cities across the country and in Canada. Once an agent receives a breakdown, they pull the pictures and resumes of actors they want to submit and send them to the casting director.

Submissions

The day the breakdown is released, hundreds of *submissions* are delivered to the casting director's office, and the long process of opening and reviewing the contents of each envelope begins. As the casting director opens each submission, he will pull out the pictures of actors with whom he is familiar and those he would like to meet.

When pulling pictures of new actors to meet, each casting director has their own specific process. Some casting directors base their selection simply on looks. That is, does the actor look like the character as envisioned in the casting director's mind? Others base their choices on a combination of looks and *credits*.

Prereads

After pulling pictures, casting directors will ask their assistant to set up a series of auditions. This allows casting directors to read new actors, or actors with whom they are familiar but are unsure if they are right for this particular role. These casting sessions are called *prereads* and involve only the actor and the casting director.

Callbacks

After a casting director has finished lists, availabilities, and prereads, he has a very good idea of which actors should audition for the producers. The casting director then begins to schedule *callbacks* (also called *producers' sessions*.) Callbacks are auditions which include the casting director, producers and director. It is at this point that the hiring decisions are made, and when casting directors are under the greatest pressure.

Negotiations

Casting directors are responsible for negotiating all actors' *contracts* (and processing the paperwork) for the project whether it be for television, stage or feature films. This can be a very simple process, but often the casting director will turn to the *business affairs* department of the studio, production company, or network when negotiating for a star's services, a deal which can become very complicated.

The casting process can take days, weeks or months dependent upon the project and, each night until the final frame of film is shot, the casting director prays that all goes well.

What Casting Directors Can Do For You

Casting directors can be very helpful by guiding you through the audition process, and opening doors to producers and directors. As we progress through each of the following chapters, we will describe in more detail how casting directors can help you and how you can help them. However, the bottom line is that each and every casting director wants to hire you the minute you walk through the door. It may be hard to believe, but it is true.

BEFORE THE AUDITION

For the beginning actor, experience is crucial. Whether it's high school, college, or community theatre, if you are performing, you are developing your talent.

While fame may be one of your ambitions, the most successful actors focus more on being good than on being famous. Training is essential to provide your career with a solid foundation. No matter how much innate talent you may be blessed with, every workshop or class you take will expose you to new ideas, techniques, and approaches that can help you improve your craft. Even the bad classes can serve as a "how-not-to" lesson. And, just because you're working doesn't mean you have nothing left to learn. Your education will never be complete: it is a career-long pursuit. Other than a strong knowledge of film and television projects, there are several tools of the trade that every actor must have. These tools not only represent you but are also a reflection of your dedication to your craft.

HEADSHOTS

The photograph (or *headshot*) is your calling card and your first introduction to a casting director. Not only must it be different enough from the thousands of other photographs a casting director will receive, but it should always accurately reflect who you are as an actor and an individual. Having the right headshot is of ultimate importance to your career.

Finding the Right Photographer

Find a professional photographer with whom you feel comfortable to take your headshots. You will use these photographs for a while, so take your time in making selections. Old yearbook photos, snapshots and Polaroids, even for children, are not professional. Meet with as many photographers as possible before making your selection. Judge carefully the quality of their work, the amount of repeat customers and the price (more expensive is not always better.) Finding the right photographer may take time but it will be worth it.

Although there are several resource guides for sale at theatre bookstores that can lead you to the right photographer, one of the best ways to find a good one is by asking friends and other actors. If you like another actor's headshot, ask the photographer's name. In addition to asking about the price, see if you can find out: Was makeup included? How many rolls of film did they shoot? Was the shoot in a studio, or on location. If on location, where and what were the arrangements? Did the photographer supply a certain number of 8 x 10s, or just proof sheets? If they have good things to report, make an appointment to see the photographer's "book" of clients.

Many actors ask their agents and acting coaches for suggestions of photographers as they see headshots all day. Be careful, however, if anyone insists that you use a particular photographer. Many unscrupulous people in town have arrangements with certain photographers that benefit both parties financially. If your agent, manager or coach insists that you use their photographer, they may be receiving a financial kickback from that photographer. If you find yourself in this situation, ask if your relationship with them is dependent upon the use of a particular photographer. If the answer is "yes," do not allow yourself to be manipulated. No legitimate industry professional will make representation dependent on such matters. Agents, managers and coaches who leave the ultimate decision up to you may just have a preference for a particular photographer's work.

Commercial vs. Theatrical Headshots

There used to be a clear distinction between commercial and theatrical headshots, but those lines are becoming blurred. In the past, commercial photographs showed wide smiles while theatrical photographs were more serious. With the advent of high fashion photography and the *real people* look, many actors have eliminated the commercial photograph completely. Listen to all your representatives' advice, and then make your decision based on your own feelings.

If you decide to have both a theatrical and commercial photograph, the two should be markedly different from each other. When you have your commercial photos taken, try various looks from studious to sexy. You will have more choices, then. Your final commercial headshot can either be a single photo of you, or a *composite* of four or five different "characters" on one 8 x 10 or 8.5 x 11 sheet. Commercial photo reproduction houses can assist you in putting together the composite if that is what you choose.

How Many and How Much?

Once you select your headshot photo, or photos, how many do you need? Ask your agent or manager, and keep within your budget. Some actors order 300 at a time in order to take advantage of price breaks; others order smaller quantities. Begin with a reasonable amount, such as 100. If you are happy with the results, you can always order more. If not, you can dump them at a relatively low loss.

Reproduction prices vary greatly. You should do serious bargain hunting. What seems inexpensive at one store may seem exorbitant at another. Again, ask around for a photo lab that specializes in multiple copies.

Qualities of Photographs

Every actor wants a perfect headshot—one that will jump out and catch the casting director's eye. Here are some things casting directors ask when reviewing photos for a role.

Does the person in the photo:

1. Resemble the character as envisioned?

2. Look the right age?

3. Match the qualities the producer is looking for? (e.g., good-looking, character, ethnicity.)

Some of the more subjective questions are:

4. Is this an accurate representation of the actor?

5. Is there something going on behind the eyes?

6. Is this an actor just striking a pose or is this who this person is?

Trying to guess what every casting director will find appealing may make you crazy. Make sure that your photograph looks like you and that you like it. You can then augment it with qualities which you can control through reproduction. Try to make your photograph a little different so that it will stand out from the others. However, be careful not to make your photo so different that it is jarring to those casting the project. Here are some areas for creativity.

Finish

Black and white glossy stock paper used to be the standard for headshots. Now actors can choose between *lithographs* (usually the most inexpensive alternative,) *glossy stock* (slightly more expensive) and *pearltone* (usually higher in price). Look at other people's photos and choose a finish that can make yours stand out by being a little different. Is glossy "in" this year? Then try a pearltone finish.

Color vs. black and white

The dramatic reduction in price of color photo reproduction seemed to predict the death of black and white headshots in the entertainment industry. This prediction did not come true as black and white 8 x 10s are still the standard in casting offices, (and even with the price drop, color photo reproduction is still pretty pricey.)

Some actors—those with red hair in particular—do choose to have their pictures reproduced in color, but it is more the exception than the rule.

Do color headshots really stand out more? Absolutely, but not always in a positive way. If you choose to use color, wear neutral clothing as bright colors may draw the casting director's eyes away from your face and to your wardrobe. Another option, although it is not necessary, is to have your black and white photos lightly hand-tinted in color. Good reproductions of these hand-colored photos can help your picture stand out.

Name on the Photograph

Should your name be on the front of the picture? Although most casting directors still prefer having your name printed on the front of your photograph, it is not a necessity. If you choose to do it, keep it simple. Block letters in an appropriate size that do not detract from your picture are your best bet. If the letters are too large or too ornate, the casting director's attention will be drawn more to your type style than to your face. Your face is what sells you. If you choose to leave your name off your photo, make sure you place it (handwritten or stamped) on the back of the photo in case your picture and resume become separated.

Agency Logo

Printing your agency's logo on the front of your photographs is still common in commercial headshots, but not so in theatrical pictures. The only drawback of having your representation printed directly on your photos is that if you change agents, you will be stuck with photos which are useless unless changed. Many actors are deleting agency representation from the front of the photo. Just make sure it is on your resume.

Borders

Borders on photos can have a positive effect on a casting director. Good use of borders can enhance your picture immensely if they

Photo / Gary Kuwahara

Jusak Yang Bernhard

Sample Headshot

LEAH REMINI

Sample Headshot

Once when casting a pilot, we were down to the wire looking for our co-lead. An actress was supposed to read for the network, but the agent and the studio's business affairs department couldn't close the deal. Three hours prior to testing at the network, the agent and business affairs finally agreed on everything. The only problem was now the actress couldn't be reached! She had no pager and no one could find her. She lost an opportunity to test and possibly work on a hit series. Always carry a pager and make sure your agent knows how to reach you. —E.K.

are used creatively. If all the headshots you see have 1/4 inch borders on all sides, try 1/2 inch borders or 3/4 inch borders. If the pictures you see have absolutely no borders (*full bleed*), go with extreme borders or place your picture at an angle within those borders. Chances are, everybody else will catch up with you eventually and you will have to change your borders in a few years in order to keep your competitive edge.

Full Face, Full Body or 3/4 Body Shot

Again, each casting director has her own preference. Full face shots are great unless everyone is doing them. Perhaps, then, it is time to try a 3/4 shot. While there are no hard and fast rules to obey, it is wise to make sure that your picture is not so different that casting directors are unable to tell what you look like. Although extreme close-up photographs are artistic, they make it hard for the casting director to judge your appearance. The same goes for profile shots. It is striking but it only shows us half of you, and who is going to take a chance on casting an actor if you don't know what the other side of his face looks like?

RESUMES

Many actors are convinced that casting directors care more about the photograph than they do about the *resume*. There is some truth to this. Casting directors first look at the photo to see if the person meets the physical requirements. If that is the case, she will immediately look at the resume. Therefore, your resume is not second in line to your picture but of equal importance.

While each actor, agent and casting director has her own ideas about the layout and look of a resume, most are in agreement as to what information is essential. As you design your resume, make sure you include the following items.

YOUR NAME—exactly as you are listed with your union and how you would like it to appear on-screen.

CONTACT INFORMATION—Agency name and telephone number, personal manager's information and your personal contact information, including your answering service, voice-mail or pager number. Including both helps to ensure that the casting director can get in contact with you for last minute auditions.

UNION AFFILIATIONS—(SAG, AFTRA, Equity) Although some agents consider these optional, most casting directors prefer that they be included on your resume, especially if you do not have much experience.

VITAL STATISTICS—Height, weight, eye-color, and age-range. Age-range (not actual age), is not absolutely necessary but some casting directors find it helpful.

FEATURE FILM CREDITS—Include project title, character name or type of role, production company or studio, and director. The year of the production is not necessary as it will date you.

TELEVISION CREDITS—Include project title, character name or type of role, production company, studio and network, and director.

THEATRE CREDITS—Include project title, character name or type of role, theatre company, and director.

COMMERCIAL CREDITS—On a theatrical resume, most actors simply put the phrase, *list available upon request*, rather than listing each credit.

SPECIAL SKILLS—Martial arts, singing, juggling, weaponry, stunts—and how adept you are at each of them. Do not overstate your skills. If you are a beginner, say so. Exaggerating your abilities can be dangerous and possibly lead to your dismissal if you are unable to perform as expected.

DIALECTS AND LANGUAGES—List all you are capable of performing and your level of fluency. Again, never exaggerate your fluency in languages.

PROFESSIONAL TRAINING—Schools, degrees, coaches.

VALID PASSPORTS—If you are a minor and/or not a resident of the United States, then list all U.S. work permits. With the increasing frequency of projects which film outside the U.S. this information becomes very important.

In order not to leave anything out, take the time to sit down and write out your credits. Once you have decided what information you are going to include, you can design the format of your resume.

While the look of your resume is always up to you, most agents have particular formats they prefer. In this chapter are some samples of a few resumes which are clear, easy to read, and properly formatted.

Resume: Size

Standard size letter paper is 8.5 x 11 inches. Standard photos are 8 x 10 inches. Should your resume be cut down to fit on the back of your 8 x 10 photo? It makes filing the pictures easier for the casting director. Whether you choose 8.5 x 11 or 8 x 10, attach your resume securely to your photo with staples (or glue, if you like). There are also many photocopy and print shops which have the ability to print your resume directly on the back of your picture. This option can save time or worries about lost resumes, but it can also prove expensive if your resume changes frequently due to work. [Note: Some higher quality photocopy machines can accept paper as thick as photo stock and print on the back. It may be worth experimenting with a few, as this is a relatively inexpensive compromise.]

Credit Order

Your most recent (or most impressive) credits should be listed first in each category.

Category Order

There is no preference for credit category order (feature film, television, stage, commercial) but you should base your decision upon the source of the majority of work available. If you live in New York or Chicago where theatre is the predominant source of work, list your theatre credits first. If Los Angeles is your home base, list your feature film credits first, followed by television and stage.

Type Style

The simpler your type style, the better. All information on your resume should be easy to read. Helvetica and Times are the world's most popular typestyles because they are clean, simple, and easy to read.

Agency Logo

Placing your agency logo on your resume certainly makes finding your representation easier for the casting director. As long as your contact information is on the resume, however, it doesn't matter whether it is simply typewritten or in logo form.

Credit Layout

Credit layout is the most important aspect of any resume because it contains all the information you want the casting director to have. We recommend the following format:

Category Title

Project Title	Role / Size of Role	Network, Studio / Director
Television:		
FRIENDS	"Mr. Wayne"/Guest Star	NBC/Warner Bros./Mac Vint
ROUNDS	"Lester"/Series Regular	FBC/Paramount./Les Lan
LIFE (MOW)	"Singh"/Lead	WBN/Warner Bros./Eric Koy

JOEY ACTOR

UNION

FILM

The Dark Corner	Mr. Laft	Dir.: V. Ramsey
Afterlife	Hugh	Dir.: John Boudreau
Doomsday	Man on Phone	Dir.: H. Simi

TELEVISION

Monster Math	Lead	NBC
Family Fries	Starring	CBS
Revolution	Guest Star	FBC
Revolution	Guest Star	FBC
Holiday Times	Guest Star	UPN
My Father the Car	Co-Star	WBN
Trashman	Featured	ABC

STAGE

My Life in Chains	Dir.: Ving Thames
Hamlet: The Musical	Dir.: Tom Tyrone

INDUSTRIALS

Prime Bell Telephone, Off-Line Computer

COMMERCIALS

Big Sucker Vacuums, Line Dry Detergent, Oil of Penz
Moisturizer

TRAINING

Improv,	Voice, Movement, Stage Combat
Schooling:	Case Western Reserve University
	University of Western Ohio

DIALECTS

Southern, British, French, Scandanavian, Yugoslavian, Russian, Irish, Italian, good ear for all dialects.

SPECIAL SKILLS

All Martial Arts, Speak French & Russian, Horseback Riding, Weaponry, Juggling, Singing, Skiing, Basketball, Football, Ping Pong, Tennis, and very fast learner at all sports.

Example of bad resume design and presentation.

Height: 5' 10"
Weight: 300 lbs.
Hair: Blonde
Eyes: Blue

JOSEPH ACTOR

SAG • AFTRA • AEA • AGVA

Service: (818) 555-5555

Big
Talent
Agency
1234 Really Big Street
Hollywood, California 90000
(213) 555-5555

FILM

The Dark Corner	Lead	Disney	Dir.:Victor Ramsey
Afterlife	Co-Star	Warner Bros.	Dir.: John Boudreau
Doomsday	Featured	Imagine	Dir.: Hal Simi

TELEVISION

Monster Math	Lead (MOW)	NBC / Columbia	Dir.: Eric Koyanagi
Family Fries	Series Regular	CBS / TriStar	Dir.: Clifford Son
Revolution	Recurring	FBC / 20th Century Fox	Dir.: Vince Neill
Holiday Times	Guest Star	UPN / Paramount	Dir.: Michael Van
My Father the Car	Co-Star	WBN / Warner Bros.	Dir.: Lace Melton
Trashman	Featured	ABC / ABC Prods.	Dir.: Robin Lunch

STAGE

My Life in Chains	Lead	Open Air Theatre	Dir.: Ving Thames
Hamlet: The Musical	Chorus	Absurdity Theatre	Dir.: Tom Tyrone

INDUSTRIALS
List available upon request

COMMERCIALS
List available upon request

TRAINING

Improv: Groundlings, Second City (LA)
Movement: Zarl Benes, Sahala Croton, Thea Mel
Schooling: Case Western Reserve University (MFA)
         University of Western Ohio (BFA)

Voice: Paul McGronth, Lisa Milargh, Tenie McGraw
Stage Combat: Maya Jasper, Pohl Vinsa, Clay Pigeon

DIALECTS

Southern U.S., Proper British, South London, French, Scandanavian, Yugoslavian, Russian, Irish, Italian

SPECIAL SKILLS

Gung Fu (Black Belt), Thai Kickboxing (Nationally Ranked), Horseback Riding (Western Saddle), Speak French
fluently, Some knowledge of Russian (beginning), Weaponry (handguns only), Juggling, Singing (Mezzo Soprano),
Skiing (expert at snow skiing & beginning water skiing), Basketball, Football, Ping Pong, and Tennis.

VALID U.S. PASSPORT
DUAL CITIZENSHIP: CANADA & U.S.

1/2" VHS Videocasette Available Upon Request

Example of good resume design and presentation.

DEMO REELS

How the casting world ever managed before the invention of videotape is a mystery for many within the entertainment industry. *Demo reels* serve multiple purposes: from securing an agent to providing proof to producers that you are suited for a particular role. Your tape can be useful before, after, or in place of an audition, as some casting directors are occasionally allowed to cast directly from demo reels (although that situation is rare.) The importance of a professional demo reel can not be understated.

A demo reel is a mini-showcase of your talent and abilities. It will reflect your work and your flexibility as an actor . . . and all in a few minutes. Here are some good guidelines:

1. Demo reels should be no longer than 10 to 12 minutes from beginning to end.

2. Your most recent or most impressive work should be showcased first on the tape.

3. Both comedic and dramatic pieces should be included, showcasing your range by presenting a variety of characters. Some actors even have separate comedy and drama demo reels.

4. Pieces that represent your physical abilities (e.g., dance, martial arts) should be included but held to a minimum, especially if you have no dialogue.

5. Include scenes in which you speak a foreign language, but don't make them the sole focus of your reel.

6. *Extra* work (nonspeaking roles) should always be left off demo reels.

7. Include only the best scene from each project. If you can't decide which is your best scene from a particular movie or show, ask someone.

8. Include a still shot of your headshot as a lead-in to the tape so that the casting director knows whom to look for.

9. A compilation of different characters you have played set to music is fine. However, do not let the music or compilation go on for more than 10 seconds as the viewer may lose interest.

10. Commercial footage on a theatrical demo tape is generally discouraged unless it is the only footage you have or you were part of a very high-profile campaign (e.g., "Got milk?")

11. Use the highest quality possible (Broadcast quality.) Copies of copies of copies should be avoided as should video from stage plays unless it was recorded by a professional videographer and includes broadcast-quality sound and picture.

12. Generally, do not include monologues in your demo reel. The only exception would be if you performed a monologue in a film or television show. The taped monologue should be of broadcast quality.

13. Don't promote another actor on your demo reel. If you feel another actor in your chosen scene eclipses your performance, you may want to eliminate it from the reel. You don't want a casting director to watch your reel and be more interested in someone else in the scene. The only exception to this follows.

14. Include any scenes you have with "stars," even if the role is very small. Being seen in a piece with Jack Nicholson is very impressive. Also, scenes from major box-office hits never hurt. These scenes will show that you are able to hold your own even when the stakes seem intimidatingly high.

After you have assembled the desired footage, take it all to a professional editing facility. The best footage in the world won't help at all if the editing is amateurish. Shop around for a good price, but don't skimp here. Each scene should have a sense of flow into the next and should be marked as coming from a separate project. For example, if your first piece of tape contains two minutes from an episode of COURTHOUSE, the title of the show should be superimposed over the very beginning of the scene, and the title of the following piece should be similarly marked.

Once your tape is edited and ready, remember the following:

1. Have multiple copies made in 1/2 inch VHS format (standard home grade video tape) and several in 3/4 inch format (for those casting directors who still use 3/4 inch machines.) Beta format is not used in casting offices.

2. Store the original (master) tape in a safe place. Never give it to anyone, no matter how important it may seem. You never want to lose your original tape as it would be very expensive and time-consuming to recreate.

3. Give several copies of the tape to your agent and your manager so they may send them out upon request.

4. Make sure that your name and contact number are clearly marked on both the tape and the tape box. If you do not mark the tape correctly (and many actors forget to put their name and phone number on them,) don't expect to ever see it again.

5. If you submit your tape to a casting director, always pick it up promptly when asked to do so by the casting office. A general rule to keep in mind is, "One call is a necessity. Two calls are a courtesy. Three calls are a bother." Many casting offices will make two calls and then automatically recycle or throw out the tape if it has not been picked up.

THE CASTING TEAM

Understanding the inner workings of a casting office can be one of the most important facets of having a good audition experience. You should know who each of the players are and exactly what they do in the office. No matter how unimportant any member of the casting team may seem to you, each should be treated with the same amount of respect.

CASTING INTERN

The lowest person on the casting totem pole (and perhaps the most underappreciated) is the *casting intern* who works for little or no pay (usually to get experience or a foot-in-the-door) and is responsible for everything, from getting lunch to standing at the fax machine for hours sending out *sides* (those pages of the script being read for a particular audition.) They work long, hard hours, often without recognition.

READER

An individual hired (although they are seldom paid) to read with auditioning actors. Readers are used for several reasons: A casting director may feel that their own acting abilities are not sufficient to help the actor do their best, or they simply may not like reading with an actor while trying to evaluate their work.

Readers are very often actors who want to see the inner workings of a casting office. In some cases, readers are actors with ulterior motives of landing a job. Although readers do not have a say in callbacks, they can help you tremendously during your audition by reading well with you.

If you decide you would like to be a reader, you must be committed to the job. From the moment you accept the responsibility, you are no longer an actor. You are not there to book a job for yourself. Most casting directors will tell actor-readers that they will not be considered for a role while working in the office. It may be frustrating being a reader, but you could gain invaluable knowledge.

CASTING ASSISTANT

Casting assistants have a great deal of work to handle—more than just answering the phones and directing you to the restrooms. They are an integral part of the casting office. They field phone calls, set audition appointments, baby-sit the actors, pamper the casting director, get yelled at by the casting director, get yelled at by the producers, get yelled at by the director, get yelled at by the agents, and are the casting director's eyes and ears when he is behind closed doors.

If you are rude to the casting assistant, be assured that the casting director will hear about it. Casting directors want nice people to work on their projects. If you cause trouble in the office, more than likely you will cause trouble on the set. With few exceptions, every casting director starts out as an assistant.

CASTING ASSOCIATE

Next in the pecking order comes the *casting associate*. In an independent casting director's office (studio casting departments rarely employ associates,) when an assistant has amassed the knowledge necessary to take an *on-line casting* position, they are promoted to the status of associate—more responsibility than an assistant, but often not more money.

When a casting director takes on several projects, she often has an associate *cover a project*. That means that the associate does the prereads, organizes the producers' sessions and essentially casts the project. The difference is that the casting director still gets the "big bucks" and on-screen credit (although, the credit can be shared with the associate,) but the associate gains the hands-on experience essential to his career development.

In some cases, you may read only for an associate before moving on to a callback for producers. Other times, you will read for the associate and then have an instant callback for the casting director. It all depends on the dynamics of each particular office. Whatever you do, keep in mind that the casting associate is just as responsible for making decisions as the casting director.

CASTING DIRECTOR

Casting directors are on your side—they want to hire you. They understand how difficult it is to be an actor. When you walk through the casting door, casting directors are hoping you are the person they are looking for. It would mean their job is done and they can move on to another role or project. [Of course, you will still have to read for the producers and director. Casting directors recommend while the producers and directors make the decision.]

There are plenty of talented actors out there, and life is too short to deal with the nasty ones. A good attitude combined with talent will always keep casting directors' minds and doors open.

When I first started out in casting, an actor was extremely rude. He refused to audition for the role he was given. He was obstinate, insisting that this was obviously a mistake on my part, as the casting director never would have offended him by bringing him in to read for such a small role.

When informed that there was no mistake, the actor became irate and, in front of a whole room of people, demanded to speak with the casting director. After a long discussion, the casting director let him read what he wanted. He was awful. It has been nearly ten years since that day, and that actor has just now been allowed back in my office. —P.B.

NEXT!

An Actors Guide
to Auditioning

TYPES OF AUDITIONS

Auditioning is an art form. Nearly every casting director and actor will tell you the same thing: you can be the most brilliant actor in the world and never book a job if you don't know how to audition. Understanding each type of audition is vital to your career. The more you audition, the easier the process will become provided you treat each audition as a learning process. Following are the various types of auditions in the order they typically occur. There are always exceptions to the order, depending upon each casting director and the status of your career.

CATTLE CALL

Imagine hordes of actors all auditioning for the same part. Once you have been on one, you will see why cattle calls, or *open calls* are appropriately named. Although they are more common when casting theatre and commercials, they are not unheard of in features and television. Launching an extensive search for "the perfect actor", the producer or casting director will place an announcement in a trade paper (e.g., *DramaLogue* or *Backstage*) seeking a certain type of actor. The announcement will include a place and time span in which everyone who shows up will be seen. The key word is "seen."

In the theatre, each actor attending the call has a better chance of being seen and read for a role. In feature and television open-calls, actors are usually seen but not read. The casting director or producer assigns you a number, takes a Polaroid picture (even if you have a professional headshot,) possibly chats with you, and then looks over the entire group. At this point, the powers-that-be chooses those individuals who fit the physical qualities they are looking for. The rest are sent home. In most cases, those left will get a chance to read some material from the script.

What is the point of an open-call if most of the people don't get to read? Simple. Casting directors and producers never want to overlook a potential star, but if you don't meet the required physical qualities, reading a scene would be a waste of everyone's time.

Occasionally casting directors are also looking for specific skills to go along with the physicality. For example, when casting a rap movie, the goal might be to find "fresh faces" who can act and rap.

Another reason cattle-calls exist is because they generate *publicity*. Producers know that shows like ENTERTAINMENT TONIGHT, E! ENTERTAINMENT TELEVISION, and EXTRA! THE ENTERTAINMENT MAGAZINE like to show up at these events, and that can substantially increase the industry "buzz" about the project.

One of the biggest open-calls ever held was for the role of "Scarlett" in the *mini-series* of the same name. It was hyped on every news program in the States for months, built up to rival the original search resulting in Vivien Leigh landing the role in GONE WITH THE WIND. Professional and amateurs lined up in casting offices and shopping malls across the country for a chance at portraying one of the most beloved literary heroines ever created. The producers wanted an unknown to play the role. Although the search was very legitimate, the actress they eventually hired was not a product of the cattlecall searches. Joanne Whaley Kilmer, who had measurable success in her career in such films as WILLOW and SCANDAL, was well-known in casting circles and was a professional actress (albeit, relatively unknown to the general public) who was submitted by her agent.

As unpleasant as cattle calls can be for both the casting director and actor, chances are you will *go* on one during your career as an actor. While you may not encounter them quite as much in film and television, you should be aware of them. The two auditions you will face most often are the *preread* and the *callback*.

PREREAD

A *preread* is a reading for the casting director (or associate) only. The casting director will listen to your reading, evaluate your suitability for a given role, and determine if you should be seen by the producers. As casting directors we are hired by the producers who don't have the time to see hundreds of actors for each role in a series, film, or mini-series.

Prereads are usually more casual and, even though you still need to be professional, you generally don't need to worry about having more than one or two people in the room. If the casting director has a partner, associate or assistant, sometimes they will sit in. If you have questions about the project, role, or character motivation this is the time to ask them. If you have questions and don't ask them, you are not giving yourself every opportunity to present a good audition.

The objective in a preread is to have your performance convince the casting directors that you are perfect for the job. Let your acting speak for you. Do your very best with the material and trust that your talent will show through.

Casting is a subjective art form, however. Just as each actor will perform a scene or interpret a character differently, ten different casting directors will cast the same role ten different ways. It all depends upon each casting director's interpretation of the character. Whether you progress to the callback may not be solely dependent upon your talent.

CALLBACK

A *callback* (or producers' session) is when you read for the casting director, the producer, the writer, the director, the star, the associate, and whomever else the producer or director wants in the room. That can be anywhere from two to ten people, depending

A wonderful actress came in several times for a sitcom pilot I was casting. Her performance was consistent and funny in each of her callbacks, and the producers decided to test her at the network. The day before the test, the actress called and said she had a different "take" on the character and wanted to try it out for us before she went to the network. The producer and I watched this new interpretation, and it was not nearly as funny as her original choice. We thanked her for her initiative, but asked her to forget her new vision of the character and go back to what we'd liked so much the first (and second, and third) time she auditioned. She did, got the part, the series became a phenomenon, and she and her five co-stars will be sitting on a couch sipping coffee for years to come when the show plays in syndication. —E.K.

on how big the part is and who is involved in the production. The other difference between a callback and preread is that this is when decisions are usually made.

If, after your preread, you receive a callback, ask your agent if the casting director has any *direction* (*adjustments*) for you. If not, then your reading was exactly what the casting director was looking for. In that case, when you read for producers, do exactly the same thing. After all, that reading is what got you the callback in the first place.

If you do receive some direction after your preread (whether directly from the casting director or through your agent), think about it. Is it clear? Is it precise? Does it make sense? If it doesn't make sense, call your agent. Maybe she can clarify it. If you still have questions, ask your agent if you may call the casting director directly. Casting directors want you to get the direction correctly so you can get the job. If the casting director has given you any type of direction, it is for a reason. The producers have told the casting director a specific way to go with the character, and the casting director wants your reading to be as close to that as possible.

If you have a considerable amount of time between your preread and callback, don't over-rehearse. It can remove any spontaneity or reality you have given the reading. Over-rehearsing can also make it more difficult for you to make any additional adjustments given to you in the callback. If you've over-rehearsed and the producer directs you, the scene may feel awkward or wrong to you with this new direction as you have become too familiar with the material. What counts is the way they want it done. You have to remain flexible.

Be consistent. If you wore a specific outfit to the preread, wear the same outfit to the callback (unless instructed otherwise). Your goal is to repeat as closely as possible your preread performance—from clothes to acting—that got you the callback in the first place.

Be prepared. The producers could ask you to read for another role, give you new information that could throw you, add an appropriate accent, or . . . . Don't be caught off guard. Rehearse the scene moving around and sitting down; practice it with an accent and without (if appropriate); familiarize yourself with the other characters. If you are given direction or a new character to read, make sure you ask for some time to look over the material before you read. You deserve the time and, in these types of situations, most producers will offer it to you. But if they don't, ask.

Other than being professional, prepared, punctual, personable, perky, relaxed, open-minded, awake, aware, sober and brilliant—just have a good attitude and do your best.

Multiple Callbacks

When auditioning for a guest appearance on episodic television or for a supporting role in feature films, you will know whether or not you were hired after the first or second audition. The process is a little longer for a feature film (or mini-series or movie of the week) or a regular role in a television series.

I once had an actor come in for a preread wearing a nice silk suit, an excellent choice because the character was very hip and slick-perfect. His reading was good, and he was given a callback. When he came in to read for the producers, he was wearing a ripped tank top, ripped bike shorts and a hat. He looked as if he had just come from the gym. When he left, my producers turned and said, "Why would an actor wear that for this kind of role?" He gave everyone the impression that he simply didn't care about the audition. —E.K.

My producers and I were thrilled that a legendary rock star was interested in a series regular role for a one-hour pilot. He'd agreed to meet, but not read. He was charming and charismatic, but his limited acting experience was a concern. We delicately asked him if he'd looked at the audition material. He hadn't but was willing to read. I suggested he spend some time with the sides, but he enthusiastically offered to read it "cold." He started beautifully, but soon tripped over the words and asked to start again. After several attempts, it was clear he wasn't going to get through the material without flubbing the lines. He grinned sheepishly and said, "I could sing it for you." We shared a laugh, and he left. Sight reading music would have been no problem for this singer, but he should have taken more time with the scene, or come back another day. By the way, he did appear on the series as a special guest star. The moral: You can misjudge your limitations, blow an audition, and still get a good part . . . if you happen to be a legendary rock star!—E.K.

The entertainment industry is a business. When launching a series or a motion picture costing millions of dollars, many individuals are responsible for making sure that the project is an artistic and financial success. Therefore, every company with a vested interest in the project is given an opportunity to approve a performer. Here are some of the situations you may encounter and tips on how you can do your best.

Second Callback for Producers

Television "guest star" and "Co-star" roles rarely have additional callbacks. Because of the time constraints, producers will usually make a decision immediately following the first session. Sometimes, however, they are torn between two performers and want to see them again. If this happens to you, just come in and do exactly what you did the first time, unless you have received a specific adjustment.

In MOWs, pilots, and features, multiple callbacks are more common due to the sheer number of actors seen by the producers. There is usually more time allowed when casting a pilot, feature or MOW; therefore, more actors are seen. Try not to make yourself crazy. It's the same job. There are just a few extra steps involved and a few more people in the room.

Let's say that you are auditioning for a role in "Made For You" a new primetime series. For any given role, a casting director will bring a group of actors in to see the producers. The producers will then narrow the list down to the three to five actors they like the best for each role. It may take multiple callbacks to get to this stage.

Chemistry Reading

If "Made For You" is considered by industry insiders as a hot project, it is likely that a star involved. If so, once the producers have decided that they like your interpretation of the character, the next step in the process may be a *chemistry reading* with the star.

In a chemistry reading, the actors up for the co-lead or supporting roles each have the opportunity to read with the star. Once the reading is over, the producers and the star evaluate the chemistry between each actor and the star. Not everyone makes it through this step. Most stars have gone through this process at some point in their careers and can be very supportive in this moment of stress.

Don't expect every star to be a saint during your chemistry reading, though. Personality conflicts between the star and an actor, the star's disapproval of the actor's abilities, or the star's realization that your talent might eclipse his own are all reasons that could put you out of the running. If you are eliminated at this point, remember that it may have absolutely nothing to do with your talent. Every casting director has seen stars sabotage other actors during chemistry readings simply out of ego.

Executive Callback (Studio Reading)

Once you make it past the chemistry reading (if, in fact you even went through that step,) there is another set of individuals waiting to give their stamp of approval. These are the studio executives— "The Suits" —and you will need to repeat your audition in front of them.

Since the studio is laying out the majority of the money and, therefore, has the most to win or lose, studio approval is an essential part of the audition process. When casting a feature film, the studio executives must approve the producer's choices. For a television pilot, mini-series or MOW, the studio will need to

NEXT!

An Actors Guide
to Auditioning

support all the producer's choices in front of the network executives. Until now, everyone you have read for has seemed very relaxed, casual and familiar. Now, you face a room full of total strangers upon whom your possible employment depends. Focus on your work, and don't be intimidated. Do it the same way you did before.

After you leave the audition, the executives will discuss how each actor interpreted the role and whether they should progress to the next step in the process. When dealing with feature films, MOWs and mini-series, the next step will probably be a screen test. If "Made For You" is a pilot, the next step is the network test. Regardless, both auditions are similar with the exception that a screen test is filmed on a sound stage and the network test is off camera in an executive's office, or a screening room.

SCREEN TEST

A screen test is used primarily for feature films, MOW's and mini-series, however with one exception, the process is exactly the same as a network test. In a screen test you will usually have makeup, wardrobe, lighting, the camera and possibly even the star added into the equation. All that external stuff can either be nerve-wracking, or incredibly helpful depending upon your outlook. Some actors, particularly stage actors in transition to film, are quite comfortable with this process and see these accoutrements as adding to their performance. Others find them a hindrance, worrying about jackets that don't fit or collars that pinch their necks. While it may seem that the casting director or producers are making the screen test as difficult as possible by adding these things, they are truly only trying to enhance the total perception of the character.

NETWORK TEST

Going to the Network is a phrase which describes the final step in the audition process when casting regular roles for series or pilots. Your agent will call to tell you when and where that reading will be.

In some instances, that test can be several weeks away or several hours depending upon the production's schedule. At this point, the process is nearly over. The only hurdle left is to get approved by the network executives. The entire process can be quite grueling if you don't keep it in perspective.

Test Option Deal (TOD)

Don't think you are going through this audition process alone. Prior to your audition for the network, and sometimes before the studio executive readings, your agent will be hard at work negotiating what is called a *test option deal (TOD)*. Essentially, your agent is pre-negotiating your salary and perks for the next five years, should the show last that long. A TOD is an important document, both for the producers and for yourself, and you can not read for the network until the TOD is done (*closed*) and signed.

A TOD is protection for you and the network. By signing a TOD before your network test, you are assured that each tiny detail of your deal is legally represented and that you have a basis for action should the network not fulfill any terms of your contract. The TOD is also an assurance for the network. If you were to read without a test option deal in place and the executives approved you, you and your agent would have all the power during negotiations. Your agent, knowing that you are the producer's choice for the job, would essentially have the network between a rock and a hard place and could demand an outrageous salary. Production companies and networks won't let themselves be put in that position and, if the TOD is not completed prior to your network or studio execs test, your audition will be canceled.

Some of the terms included in a TOD are your *pilot salary* (usually higher than your *per episode salary,*) per-episode salary, yearly raises (*bumps,*) your obligations, your *merchandising fee* (if they make an action figure of you, for example,) the number of work days, the network's right to fire you, the number of days the network has following the test to inform you whether or not you got the job, and much more. It is a lengthy document which you should read and must sign. It is important to keep in constant contact with your agent. Check your machine frequently (or carry your beeper if you own one) and ask your agent if you have questions about the content of the TOD.

The process of getting a TOD in place can be incredibly time consuming or unbelievably fast. Once your agent knows that you are going to the network, the casting director will request your quote. Your quote, the details of your last TOD, is important because that will become the basis for the casting director's (or business affairs representative's) initial offer to your agent for the current test option deal.

If you have never been through a network test before, your agent will tell the casting director that you don't have a quote while drawing their attention to any other high points in your career that may influence them to make a better offer to you (e.g., a Tony Award may cause the initial offer to be higher). The casting director will pass this information on to the producers or business affairs and formulate an offer which is open to negotiation.

If you have tested for a series before, your agent will pass on every detail of that deal to the casting director. The casting director will confirm the accuracy of that quote with the production company responsible for your last deal and then base their offer upon that quote. Again, the negotiations that follow will sometimes match your quote sometimes not; and in very rare occasions, exceed your quote.

Now the big day comes. You drive through the gates of the network and head off to the executive building with the big logo on the front. When you get to the office you will see familiar faces in the hallway—producers, casting director, the other actors, director, and sometimes the star. You may detect some tension among them. The casting director or assistant will then pull you off to the side. It's time to sign the TOD (you must do this before going in to read). Look over this document carefully before you sign it. You should have seen some version of it beforehand. Make sure that the major points your agent discussed with you are correct. If you have any questions about the document's accuracy, ask the casting director if there's a phone available to call your agent. If there are any changes to be made, make sure you discuss them with your agent and the casting director. Once all is settled, sign, sit and relax.

As the appointed time draws near, you will see a parade of unfamiliar faces file into a big room and the producers will follow. These are the network executives who include the President of the Network, Vice President of Casting, the Director of Casting, Manager of Casting, Vice Presidents of Development and more. Remember, these people also work very hard and try to do their job as best as they can. So relax, go in and do your job. Think only about doing the exact same reading that got you this far and you'll do fine. Most of all . . . don't forget to breathe.

After your test, wait until the casting director tells you that you're released. Then go out to lunch, dinner, surfing, lawn bowling, anything except go home and sit by the phone. (But don't forget your pager!) You did your job and in a few days you'll know whether you got it or not.

If you got it, congratulations. If not, don't beat yourself up or take it as a comment on your talent. You know you're talented and so does everyone whom you have met so far, otherwise you wouldn't have gotten this far. There's always the next gig. This is easier to say than do, and any depression that follows is understandable—just don't dwell on it. It was a tough road to get there but you got that far. You will get that far again.

MEMORANDUM AGREEMENT FOR TEST
WITH PILOT AND SERIES OPTION
(Subject To Closing of Network License Fee)

Date: *January 11, 2010*
Performer   *Paul G. Bens*
Role: *"Slim Jones"*
If Loanout, Name of
Corporation: *Thumbless Prods. 95-00000000*
Series/Program Title: *"Made For You" Prod. No: 12345678*
Date of Test / Interview:

Approximately January 15, 2010. After test at network, Producer has ten (10) business days to notify performer whether we will exercise option agreement.

Transportation and Expenses (if applicable):

One (1) Coach, Round Trip Airline ticket CVG/LAX/CVG, plus hotel plus $53 per diem. Round trip ground transportation to and from airport, meetings and test.

PILOT
(If Producer Exercises Pilot Option)

Title: *MADE FOR YOU*

Prod. No.   *12345678*

Length: *30 Minutes*

Approximate Start Date: *February 1, 2010*

Salary

$25,000 for eight days plus two nonconsecutive loop days.

Transportation and Expenses (if applicable)

One (1) first class round trip airfare, if used, plus hotel plus $53 per diem plus reimbursement of ground transportation to and from CVG airport plus rental car.

Dressing Room

Performer to receive a first-class, private dressing room

Sample Test Option Deal Memorandum

RESIDUALS

U.S. & Canada	SAG Minimum
Theatrical Use:	SAG Minimum
Foreign TV:	SAG Minimum
Supplemental Market:	SAG Minimum

CREDIT

Billing in the second position on a separate card in the main titles.

SERIES
(If Producer Exercises Series Option)

Tentative Series Title: MADE FOR YOU

Series Option Period:

Firm through June 25, 2010. Producer will have an option (exercisable by close of business, June 26, 2010) to extend through December 25, 2010 upon onetime payment of $5,000.

Guarantee:

Producer guarantees Performer, pay-or-play, the minimum number of episodes in each contract year as specified below. In addition thereto, Producer shall have the election to assign Performer to perform in additional episodes at the applicable episodic fee for that contract year. Beyond the guaranteed minimum, however, Producer is obligated to compensate Performer only for those episodes for which he actually renders services unless Performer is "all shows produced."

Series Sales Bonus (if applicable):

Performer to receive a onetime only series sales bonus of $5,000 provided Performer's series option is exercised.

CONTRACT YEAR—30 MINUTES

*First:	Minimum of 7 (all shows produced)
Second:	Minimum of 13 (all shows produced)
Third & Subsequent:	Minimum of 22 (all shows produced)

*In the first contract year, Producer may treat pilot as one episode.

Sample Test Option Deal Memorandum—cont'd.

If Producer makes multi-segment episodes, each segment will constitute one episode for purposes of this guarantee, and one episodic salary will be payable for each such segment.

Option date for renewal contract years

Not later than thirty (30) days after network pickup or June 1st, each year, whichever occurs sooner.

Dressing Room

Performer to receive a first-class, private dressing room.

EPISODIC SALARY—CONTRACT YEAR 30 MINUTES
(5 years; 5 1/2 if Mid-Season Start)

1	$16,500
2	$20,000
3	$27,500
4	$30,250
5	$33,275
6	$36,603

Transportation, Expenses and/or Relocation (if applicable)

If Producer exercises Performer's series option, Performer to receive a one-time only relocation fee of $5,000; one (1) first class round trip airfare per season, if used.

RESIDUALS

U.S. & Canada:	SAG Minimum
Theatrical Use:	SAG Minimum
Foreign Television:	SAG Minimum
Supplemental Market:	SAG Minimum

CREDIT

Same as Pilot

Rights, Services, etc

Performer grants Producer all rights in his services, name, likeness etc., in connection with the episodes hereunder and promotion, publicity, exhibition and exploitation thereof. Producer owns all rights in the role, the series and each episode.

Exclusivity

Maximum permitted by SAG, including time and sponsor protection.

NEXT!
An Actors Guide
to Auditioning

Sample Test Option Deal Memorandum—cont'd.

Commercials

Performer will do program commercials only, at 200% of SAG scale. Residuals at scale.

Trailers, etc

Performer will do standard openings, closings, leads, etc., at no additional compensation and series and episodic trailers at minimum compensation, if any, required by SAG, or none if none required by SAG. Performer will, subject to his availability, make promotional and institutional appearances at no additional compensation.

Consents:

Performer specifically consents to: (i) fly in chartered aircraft when required by Producer; (ii) use of his name, photograph and/or likeness in commercial publications relating to the series and any episode thereof; and (iii) use of his name, photograph and/or likeness on albums or jacket covers of commercial recordings relating to the series whether or not his performances are contained therein.

Laws, etc:

If any of these provisions are contrary to law, they will be modified to conform. Performer will abide by Producer's "Morals" and "Anti-Payola" provisions.

Producer's Remedies, etc

Producer shall have the maximum rights available at law, equity and per SAG for Performer's incapacity or default or for production interruptions due to causes beyond Producer's control. The Pilot and Series Option Periods and Option dates for Renewal Contract Years may be extended by Producer by a period equal to all or any part of the period of any production interruptions due to causes beyond Producer's control, or suspension hereunder. If the network program order is reduced because of any such events, Producer may correspondingly reduce its guarantee hereunder subject to recall of Performer upon 30 days prior written notice reducible to 10 days if no conflict with any other commitment previously made by Performer at same episodic salary if production of such unproduced program(s) is thereafter resumed.

SPECIAL PROVISIONS

Merchandising:

Five percent (5%) reducible to two and one-half (2 1/2%) in character only. In addition to Producer's merchandising rights in connection with Pilot and/or Series hereunder, subject to Performer's existing commitments, Producer shall have a 30-day right of first negotiation and a 10-day right of first refusal for merchandising rights to Performer's name, voice and likeness in connection with com-

Sample Test Option Deal Memorandum—cont'd.

modities, products or services other than those in connection with the Pilot and/or Series hereunder.

For all Schedule 'F' Performers, compensation hereunder shall be deemed payment in full for all services rendered during the entire period of production, including, but not limited to, forced calls, meal penalties and overtime. At such time as Performer reaches money breaks set forth in Section 58, compensation shall be deemed to include prepayment for looping, retakes, etc., as set forth therein.

Section 14 of the SAG-TV Agreement shall govern this agreement in respect to work time and overall production time. At such time that Performer reaches the money breaks specified in Section 14 (b), Producer will have one calendar year within which to complete all episodes ordered for the respective broadcast season.

It is contemplated that a more formal agreement will be executed by the parties which will include the above terms as well as those customarily included in agreements of this type. Until such more formal agreement is so executed, this document shall constitute the agreement between the parties.

AGREED:	REALLY BIG PRODUCTION
Thumbless Productions,	COMPANY (Productions)
95-00000000	Agent: Bigger Agent Agency
Corporation/Lender	12345 Film Street, Suite 1000
California	Star City, CA 91234
State of County of Origination	
By: _____	Attention: Iman Agent
Title: _____	Phone: 310/555-9999
	FAX: 310/555-9998

_____
Performer: PAUL G. BENS

Performer's Contract Address:
12345 Film Street
Los Angeles, CA 90000
Phone: 213/555-0000
Social Security No: 123-45-6789

Sample Test Option Deal Memorandum—cont'd.

GETTING YOUR FOOT IN THE DOOR

Now that you better understand the process, all you need is to get that first audition. Provided you have the talent, commitment, and drive to succeed in a business ripe with rejection, there are several avenues you can follow to get through the door. Some are easier, and some are more professional. All have one goal in common: an audition with the casting director.

AGENT/MANAGER SUBMISSION

If you are represented by a talent agent or personal manager, your job becomes a little easier. Typically, a casting director will release a breakdown to the agents who then submit actors whom they feel are appropriate. Trust your agent. If you are remotely right for a role (and many times when you are absolutely wrong for it,) your agent will submit your photo. That doesn't mean the casting director will see it and say, "She's the one. Let's hire her." Your agent or manager will have to go through an additional step known as the *pitch*. They will call and try to convince the casting director that you are *the* actor for the role and we just *have* to see you. If that fails, they'll beg, borrow or steal to get you that audition. Sometimes casting directors are easy to convince—sometimes not. Being an agent is a tough job—remember that.

You are a partner with your representation and you have work to do as well, not just sit by the phone and wait for it to ring. When you hear about a role that you might be right for, call your

Because of continued persistence in the face of adversity, a Los Angeles actress has become one of the hardest working women in Hollywood. After having been with a very high-profile agency for many years, she was astonished to find the number of auditions had dropped dramatically. She and her agents mutually decided that the agency would continue to field phone calls while the actress looked for new representation.

She took a very positive approach while searching for new representation by submitting herself for roles. She sent postcards, mailed photographs and resumes, and politely followed up with phone calls. Not everyone was receptive, but the auditions started coming in—*pouring in*, actually. She not only booked almost all of the jobs for which she auditioned, but also caused the rebirth of her relationship with her agency. Both realized that they needed to work together. She is living proof that persistence is essential. You can succeed, even without an agent. —P.B.

agent and tell them about it, especially if you have a prior working or personal relationship with the casting director. Chances are your representation already knows about it and has sent your picture and resume. If not, you've just given them an important piece of information. If they have submitted you, duplicating the submission by sending your picture yourself can only help. The casting director will then see your face anywhere from one to three times which may help them to remember you.

SUBMITTING YOURSELF

If you are not represented by an agent or manager, getting an audition may be a little trickier but not impossible. It takes a little more effort on your part. When you hear about a role, send in or drop off your headshot and resume as soon as possible. Remember that "drop off" actually means "drop it off and leave." Do not loiter; do not ask to see the casting director; do not ask for an audition. Casting offices are generally very busy places with tightly scheduled days. Any disruption to that schedule can be very frustrating. Persistence is fine but being too pushy can work against you. Trust that the casting director will see your submission (most casting directors tend to be very meticulous about

FROM THE DESK OF . . .
PAUL G. BENS, JR.

Dear Ms. Kanner:
Please consider me for the role of *Young Mr. Spock* in **"Star Trek 12: The Adventure Is Still Going."**
Sincerely,

Paul G. Bens, Jr.
Paul G. Bens, Jr.

Example of Submission Letter

opening every submission) and will call you with an appointment if they are interested.

One important yet often overlooked part of submitting yourself is to make sure to include a note with your photo and resume. Your note should request a *general interview* or an audition for a specific role. This should be a standard practice every time you send your materials to a casting director. Three page letters detailing your life and times since leaving the womb are not necessary and are very time consuming, not only for the casting director but for you, as well. The shorter, the better . . . even a Post-It™ will do. Also, remember to put your contact information on your resume and your picture (in case they get separated) because the casting directors can't call you if they don't have your number.

Once your photograph is in the office, it can take anywhere from one second to one day before we see it. Don't rush from the casting director's office to the nearest pay phone to check your answering machine or to call the casting director. In fact, it may not happen at all. This is where persistence comes in. Wait at least one day and follow up with a phone call. Please be professional and prepared to speak only to the casting assistant. Be kind, charming and brief. Trust that the assistant (who has been instructed to handle all calls of this nature) will pass on the message to the casting director.

AUDITION CRASHING

Audition crashing—the practice of showing up for an audition without an official appointment—is not uncommon in film and television but happens most frequently in commercial casting. While audition crashing can prove that you have the tenacity to succeed in the entertainment industry, it can also prove to be very risky. For every story of successful audition crashing that you hear, there are ten unsuccessful ones.

A young actor, upset when he didn't get a callback for a particular role, felt the casting director didn't give him a fair chance. He knew when the producers' session would take place and was planning to crash that audition. After all, he *really* wanted the part.

It was understandable to be upset, but if he crashed the producers' casting session he would make a serious mistake that could be fatal to his relationship with that casting director and his agent. All actors who went through the preread had the same chance. The casting director just didn't see what she wanted in him. Ultimately, I convinced him not to crash the audition. Although he did not get that particular role, he is currently a regular on a network television series. —P.B.

If you do choose to crash a preread, be prepared for the worst: You could be instructed to leave, banned from any future auditions with that casting director, have your agent angry at you, and call your behavior unprofessional. On the other hand, the casting director could let you read, although this is extremely rare. It all depends on the casting director's schedule, mood, generosity, desperation and your attitude.

After the prereads, the casting director carefully orchestrates the session of actors to be presented to the producers. Much thought is given to these sessions because the casting director is putting his or her reputation on the line. Once in that session, the casting director is under a lot of stress and pressure. If someone uninvited shows up, it can throw off the timing for the entire session.

Audition crashing is not recommended under any circumstances. The risks far outweigh the benefits. If you still choose to do this—proceed at your own risk.

QUESTIONS TO ASK ABOUT THE AUDITION

Good journalists know that if a story doesn't answer who, what, when, where, why (and how), it's not a good story. Slightly modified, the same holds true for a successful audition. Knowing the answers to those basic questions is a major part of any audition. When you get that call from your agent or manager telling you about an audition, what do you do? Be prepared as you would for any interview.

Before you walk in the casting office, get as much information as possible from your agent, manager, or their assistants. Here is a sample checklist of questions to ask.

FOR WHOM ARE YOU AUDITIONING?

While most times you will be reading only for the casting director, it is very important that you find out who else will be there. It can be very embarrassing when you walk in expecting only one person and there are actually seven. It can be even more embarrassing if you end up reading for the writer, director and producer and, unfamiliar with the show, you innocently ask, "Is SEINFELD a comedy?"

When you are scheduled for an audition, find out exactly who will be there, their full names and official titles. Names are especially important, not only for that particular audition, but also for the future. Write this information down and keep it on file even if you don't book the job. Their names may come up again and again throughout the course of your career.

As a quick recap and checklist:

PREREAD
Casting Assistant: _____

Casting Associate: _____

Casting Director: _____

CALLBACK/PRODUCER SESSION
Casting Associate: _____

Casting Director: _____

Producer(s): _____

Director: _____

Writer(s): _____

EXECUTIVE CALLBACK
Casting Associate: _____

Casting Director: _____

Executive Producer(s): _____

Producer(s): _____

Director: _____

Writer(s): _____

Star: _____

Studio Executives:
V.P./Head of Casting: _____

Director of Development: _____

Vice President: _____

President: _____

NETWORK TEST
Casting Associate: _____

Casting Director: _____

Network Test, cont'd.

Executive Producer(s): _____

Producer(s): _____

Director: _____

Writer(s): _____

Star: _____

Studio Executives

V.P./Head of Casting: _____

Director of Development: _____

Vice President: _____

President: _____

Network Executives

V.P./Head of Casting: _____

Director of Casting: _____

Manager of Casting: _____

Director of Development: _____

V.P. Programming: _____

President: _____

WHAT MATERIALS YOU NEED

Many actors cheat themselves by not getting the necessary materials needed to do their best; or, they get them too late. Get a copy of the breakdown, sides and script (if available.) Giving yourself as much time as possible to become familiar with them can only help you.

Breakdown

A *breakdown* is a description of the characters and plot of a given project and is generally released by casting directors to all agents. Breakdowns can give you clues as to what the casting director is looking for. Your agent can usually provide you with a copy and, as an example, we have provided a copy of a general breakdown for your perusal.

Sides

Sides are those pages of the script which contain the scenes or lines you are auditioning for. They are almost always available the day before your audition. Get them as soon as they are available, even if it means driving across town in rush hour traffic.

In this age of technology, access to a fax machine can make obtaining sides incredibly convenient. When starting a project, many casting directors will fax the sides to your agent, who can then fax them to you. If you don't have a fax machine, find a friend who does or start saving for one. Also, there are some casting directors who use Showfax or FilmFax—it does cost a fee, but their offices may be more conveniently located to you. Have your agent check with the casting director. There are also many stores and print shops which have public faxes available, just make sure that you get all the pages you are supposed to get. Having sides faxed can be especially helpful if there are any last minute changes in the material.

Script

Under SAG guidelines, a script must be made available to every actor. While this rule is difficult to enforce, most casting directors will allow access to a script (unless it isn't finished or it's a Woody Allen film.) You are entitled to ask for it. In many cases, most agents will obtain a copy of the script from the casting director at the start of the project. When you receive an audition call, ask your agent if they have the script and ask to look at a copy. Just because you ask doesn't mean you'll get your own personal copy. If you don't get to take a script home, a casting director may allow you to sit in the office and read a copy. Do it. Take the extra half-hour to two hours as it can only help your audition. This way you will better understand what the character and project are all about, especially if the script is an unfamiliar film or TV pilot.

WHEN SHOULD YOU BE THERE?

The date and time of your audition are essential. Be on time for your audition! Make sure it's the correct day. As an actor, you may not realize that a casting director has scheduled their day very carefully and any delays can throw off their whole day.

In prereads, casting directors will often stack the session. They will schedule anywhere from one to three actors every fifteen minutes within a three hour period. That is a lot of actors to see—so, if one is late it can set off a chain reaction. Casting directors hate to walk out of their offices to find they are an hour behind in their readings. Many times, it is due to tardy actors. Sometimes it is the casting director's fault, too. They may have scheduled too many actors, or been delayed by phone calls or lengthy meetings. Most times, delays are caused by circumstances beyond their control. Most casting directors will apologize for long waits. So should you, if you are late.

If you are aware before your audition that you are going to be late, call your agent. They can let the casting office know and possibly reschedule you. Do not just show up whenever you're available. Many actors show up at lunch time saying they weren't available at their audition time and could they read now? They have put the casting director in an awkward situation. The actor may get a chance to read but the casting director probably won't be happy about it.

Be on time or early for a callback. There are usually three or four producers and a director who have given the casting director

Once I brought in a well-known actress to read for a sitcom pilot. She was right for two of the roles, but only one appealed to her. First she read for the role she wanted (she was very good) then she read for the other role. The producers liked her second audition much better. When it came time to test at the network, she insisted she was better suited for the first role. Although they disagreed, the producers didn't want to lose her for both roles. They finally agreed to let her test at the network for the role of her choice, figuring if she didn't get one role, they could still offer her the other. Sure enough, she went to the network and nailed it. This doesn't happen often. In fact, it is usually the producers who end up convincing the actor. But in this case, her instincts were right. Now every week America loves her in the role she knew was best for her. —E.K.

only an hour of their time. When that hour is up, those producers are gone. If you have missed your appointed time, you may not be seen.

In any audition, it is always best to be early. This way, casting directors don't get nervous about time constraints, and you benefit from the extra time to relax and clear your mind of the day's worries. You'll do your best work that way and increase your chances of booking the job.

WHERE ARE YOU GOING?

Place and directions are the most often confused details of an audition. Many actors have gotten lost and never made it to their audition. Make sure you have the correct audition date, time and place (the location of a callback is often different than the location of the preread) as well as some type of a city map to which you can refer. (A Thomas Guide mapbook is incredibly handy.) If you are going to be late because of car trouble or wrong directions, let your agent know so they can tell the casting director. Otherwise you are going to get there and everyone will be gone . . . and so will the job.

WHY YOU SHOULD ASK QUESTIONS

After you have read the breakdown, sides and script, don't be afraid to ask any lingering questions you may still have. Most casting directors would rather you ask every question before you come in (especially if you're going straight to the producers). Don't wait until you have worked on the piece for three days only to be told—at the audition—that the character is completely different from what you thought. If you have questions, all you have to do is call your agent and have them call the casting office. They will either respond to your agent, or directly to you ASAP.

Style of the Project

What if you're not familiar with the show? Ask what the style of the project is. If you're reading for MARRIED WITH CHILDREN, a broad half-hour comedy, and you read the sides as if doing the television version of KING LEAR, you haven't done your homework. Give yourself every advantage to do your best work by knowing the style of the particular show. If the show hasn't aired yet, ask your agent.

See as many films and television programs as you can. Watch every new series at least once, especially at the beginning of each television season. This is your business—study it well.

Video stores are extremely helpful in preparing for your auditions, as you can find anything there, from long gone television series to the most current blockbusters. Videos are an indispensable source of information. Find the director's latest film. Watch the style, not only of the filmmaking but also of the acting. What's interesting about it? What actor do you remember the most? What quality drew you to that actor? Chances are, what you see in that actor is what stood out to the director. Even though the style of this film may vary from the one you're reading for, a video can clue you into the director's taste (or, sometimes, lack thereof.)

As useful as videotapes are, however, they are only a tool to understanding the particular style of a project. You must be true to your abilities and talent. You are a unique actor who has his own style of acting. Bring that essence into every role. While instances of another's work may be appealing, copying them is a disservice to you.

Name of the Project and Character

Make sure you know the name of the project and the character you are reading for. Your agent will generally have all this information, but sometimes mistakes happen. When you pick up the sides, read them through and, if something seems wrong (e.g., the character is twenty years older than you are), ask your agent or a member of the casting office if you have the correct material.

There have been times when people who were a bit too old or young for the role have been brought in to read anyway. Often it can give the casting director a sense of the actor's abilities. Who knows, perhaps the casting director may be able to use them in something else down the line.

Dressing Appropriately

Determine whether you need to dress a certain way for the role. While this doesn't necessarily mean dressing as the character, it may mean dressing appropriately. When you're reading for the new resident physician on ER, you don't want to show up wearing bicycle shorts. If being prepared means throwing several outfits in your car for two or three different auditions on the same day, do it.

As for *dressing the part*, if it will help you get into character and augment your audition, then feel free. However, if you think your "costume" is distracting to you or the people watching your audition, don't wear it.

Casting Director's Background

Another helpful thing to ask is the casting director's background. Knowledge is power in this industry, and by being aware of other projects the casting director has or is casting, you will gain some insight into that casting director's taste.

AUDITION CHECKLIST

Date _____ Time _____ Project _____ Role _____

Character Description/Questions To Ask

Audition Location _____ Audition Location Phone _____

Casting Director _____ Associate _____ Assistant _____

Producer(s) _____ Director _____

Directions _____

Appropriate Dress _____ Work Dates _____

SIDES AVAILABLE AT (if different than audition location) _____ AVAILABLE UNTIL _____ PHONE _____

☐ Television
- ☐ 1/2 Hour Pilot
- ☐ 1 Hour Pilot
- ☐ Pilot Presentation
- ☐ 1/2 Hour Episodic
- ☐ 1 Hour Episodic
- ☐ MOW/Mini-Series

- ☐ Series Regular/Lead
- ☐ Recurring
- ☐ Guest Star
- ☐ Co-Star
- ☐ Featured
- ☐ Under 5
- ☐ Voice Over

☐ Commercial
- ☐ Union ☐ Nonunion
- ☐ National
- ☐ Regional
- ☐ Buy-out

- ☐ Principal
- ☐ Featured
- ☐ Voice Over

☐ Film
- ☐ Union ☐ Nonunion
- ☐ Low Budget
- ☐ Schedule F
- ☐ Student Film

- ☐ Lead
- ☐ Supporting
- ☐ Co-Star
- ☐ Featured
- ☐ Under 5
- ☐ Voice Over

☐ Theatre
- ☐ Equity
- ☐ Equity Waiver

- ☐ Production Contract
- ☐ Guest Artists Contract
- ☐ Lort A
- ☐ Lort B
- ☐ Lort B+
- ☐ Lort C
- ☐ 99 Seat Plan

Audition Type
- ☐ Preread   ☐ Videotaped
- ☐ Callback
- ☐ Executives Callback
- ☐ Chemistry Reading
- ☐ Network Test/Screen Test

Materials
- ☐ Breakdown
- ☐ Sides
- ☐ Script Pages: _____

Network/Studio/Prod. Co.
- ☐ ABC
- ☐ CBS
- ☐ NBC
- ☐ FBC
- ☐ HBO
- ☐ WB (The Warner Bros. Network)
- ☐ UPN (United Paramount Network)
- ☐ PBS
- ☐ Other: _____
- ☐ Studio: _____
- ☐ Prod. Co: _____

NOTES/RESULT/FEEDBACK

_____

_____

_____

_____

Thank You Note Sent? _____

Sample Audition Checklist

IN THE CASTING OFFICE

Getting through the casting door is only one small step in the overall journey of getting the job. Actually booking the job can be maddening, frustrating, nerve-racking, intense, and that's just while you are waiting in the office to audition. Add in the stresses that the casting team is dealing with and that room can become a potboiler.

Following are some very basic rules or guidelines that will not only lower your stress level, but also that of the casting staff. If you keep these in mind each time you are sitting in the waiting room, you will find that you will do better once you are in the audition.

WATCH YOUR WORDS
You must be careful to watch what you say while you're in the waiting area. You never know who is there. If you think the script you're reading is bad, keep that thought to yourself.

Don't express any negative feelings you may have about any other project or person while you are waiting to audition. Not only will it drain you of the positive energy you should have for

A young actor waiting to read for producers in my office made an offhand remark to another actor that the script was awful. He didn't realize that the writer/director was standing within earshot. When he walked into the reading room and discovered his *faux pas*, it was too late. If you do not particularly care for a role or a project, keep it to yourself. Better yet, if you really dislike the project, pass on the audition. —P.B.

an audition, but you never know who will misunderstand what or whom you are talking about.

I recently brought an actress in to meet the producers on a pilot I was casting. I had previously hired her in a similar role. She felt the role was hers and proceeded to tell this to everyone in the waiting room—from other actors auditioning for the same part, to the producers, when she came into read for them. By telling everyone this was her part, she put too much pressure on herself and psyched herself out. Needless to say, she did not get the part.—E. K.

PSYCHING OUT THE COMPETITION

Psyching out the competition is very common in casting offices. Some actors do not realize they are doing it, and others have raised it to an art form, building their careers on the results. Being aware of what you are saying and what others are saying can help you avoid this pitfall.

Common Psych-Out Phrases

"What are *you* doing here?"

"God, we're such different 'types'."

"I don't understand why *you're* up for this role."

"God, you haven't worked in a while, have you?"

"I just finished a *huge* movie with . . ."

"Well, you might as well go home. Ha. Ha."

If you find yourself being "psyched out," excuse yourself from the conversation and focus on your material. Go somewhere nearby until you're called to read. (Make sure you tell the assistant where you'll be.) It is your audition and you have every right to be there and to do your best, despite what another actor may think.

If you find yourself knowingly or unknowingly psyching out another actor, stop yourself immediately and focus on you. If you are intentionally psyching out someone, you are being incredibly unfair to the other actor, and a casting assistant does notice these things. Most casting director's frown on this practice. It could influence their decision about a possible callback.

NEXT!

An Actors Guide
to Auditioning

SILENCE IS GOLDEN

In any casting office you will undoubtedly run into other actors whom you know or see on a regular basis and you may want to talk with them. This is, of course, perfectly acceptable unless the volume level in the waiting area becomes too great.

Be aware of how loudly you are speaking. If you want to have a conversation with another actor, be considerate of those who may be looking over their material and concentrating on their audition. Also be sensitive to the fact that while you are waiting, another person is reading for the casting director in the other room. Nothing is more frustrating than being in a reading that is constantly overshadowed by noise from the outer office.

Treat others with the same respect with which you wish to be treated. After all, everything that goes around, comes around. Common sense, perhaps, but often overlooked in Hollywood.

CLEANLINESS IS NEXT TO GODLINESS

Most casting offices are very clean when actors walk in, but look like a cyclone hit when they leave. Empty water cups litter the floor, pages of sides are left on chairs, and magazines are strewn about. At the end of the day, the office has more than that "lived-in look." Actors are nervous or focusing on their work but you need to pick up after yourself before walking out the door.

HAVE EVERYTHING YOU NEED

Time is of the essence in a casting office and having everything you need at arms length makes the entire process easier for everyone. Bring whatever you need with you, remembering not to leave it in the car. Some of the essentials often forgotten include the following:

Sides

The casting office may have extra sets handy, but remember, those sides won't be highlighted or contain any notes you may have made.

Photograph and Resume

Always keep some on hand. Most actors assume that their agent or manager has sent their picture and resume to the casting director. Nine times out of ten they have. There are times, though, when the casting director doesn't have your picture and resume or has misplaced it.

Script

If you have a copy of the script and were requested to return it to the casting director, do it. Return it in exactly the same condition as when it was handed to you (make sure pages are in the correct order and that none is missing.) Script photocopying is one of the biggest expenses casting directors incur (especially in low-budget feature films) and, if they ask for the script back, it is usually to keep those costs down.

Demo Reel

Have a copy of your current reel with you in case the casting director asks to see some of your other work. It is not absolutely necessary however that you bring one with you for every audition.

USE YOUR COMMON SENSE

Common sense is the most important gift and the most underused talent an actor can have. If you have any questions about whether your actions are appropriate or inappropriate, assume they are inappropriate. You can't go wrong that way. A few common sense items include:

Don't Monopolize the Telephone

While the telephone is the busiest office machine, most casting offices will either have an extension phone available for actors or allow you to use their own. Always ask to use the phone and keep all conversations brief.

Focus on Your Material

There is usually a waiting period from the time you arrive until you actually audition for the casting director. Sometimes this waiting time is excruciatingly long. Make the best possible use of this time by focusing on your material and your work. If you spend all your time chatting with others you are cheating yourself (and them) of an opportunity to prepare.

No Snooping Allowed

Many casting offices may have multiple projects going simultaneously. You may see sides, scripts, and even partially completed contracts lying around on the casting director or assistant's desks. These materials are not for your perusal. Those desks and the items on them are private areas as far as actors are concerned. If you happen to see something you shouldn't, do not mention it to anyone.

When reading for a part, many actors will see sides for other characters and decide that they would rather read for one of those roles because it is "bigger" or "better." This is a tricky area. You are there to read for a specific character. If the casting director thinks you are more appropriate for another character or project, they will ask you to read for it. If you do request to read for another role, you must be willing to accept the casting director's decision if it is no.

Listen

Pay attention to what the casting director, associate or assistant tells you, whether it be a request to lower the volume of your voice or an audition tip. Remember that knowledge is power but only when you listen to what is being said.

IN THE AUDITION

Not everything that happens in the casting office will always go as smoothly as you want it to. What will help you is knowing how to deal with different situations when something goes wrong. Below are some situations you may face and possible ways of dealing with them.

LETTING GO OF STRESS

Once you've gotten an appointment to read for a casting director or producers, walking through the door should be the easiest part of the audition process. However, many circumstances which create tremendous stress can affect your audition. You will need to find ways to let it go.

Traffic and parking seem to be the most common threats to a successful audition, especially in Los Angeles and New York. There is nothing more maddening than being stuck in bumper-to-bumper traffic only to arrive at the studio and not be able to find a parking space. By this time you are late and your demeanor can be understandably rattled.

As far as traffic is concerned, the best advice is to assume that every street will be jammed. Factor in more than enough time to weave your way through it all so that you have a few moments to relax before your audition. It is better for your state of mind to be overly early, than frustratingly late.

Lack of parking, on the other hand, does have a few remedies. Under SAG guidelines, production companies must supply sufficient

parking for auditioning actors or must make talent aware of available off-street parking. Make sure that you or your agent ask the casting office about available parking so that you know what type of delay, if any, to expect.

If you face any of these obstacles, pleasantly inform the assistant of insufficient parking or bad traffic conditions, and then focus on your material. If you have had a difficult day because of family pressures, financial problems or the like, let go of all that the second you walk in a casting director or producer's office. Although this is easier said than done, with a little practice you will find ways to let go of it all.

Once you have arrived at the audition location, you should have little trouble finding or gaining access to the office. Disabled actors may find more barriers to a positive audition experience. Under the *Americans with Disabilities Act*, all public buildings are required to be accessible to the handicapped. Not every landlord adheres to this mandate which can be a hindrance when booking a job. If you are handicapped, your agent should always tell the casting director when scheduling your audition. If the building is not accessible, the casting director can often make special arrangements with the production office or studio before your audition. If, however, you find this out only upon your arrival, locate the nearest phone and contact your agent, the casting director or studio security to ask for assistance. If they are unable to help, you have every right to request a rescheduled audition time at an accessible location. If a casting office is unwilling or unable to reschedule your audition, consult your union official.

FIRST IMPRESSIONS

The first time you meet a casting director or producer is extremely important. A good first impression can set the entire tone for any future relationship with them. A bad one can eliminate the chances of making a second impression. While letting go of the pressures of the day is one way to ensure a positive reaction, there is another trap actors can unintentionally fall into that can cause some damage.

Arriving *in character* is a method many actors employ as preparation for an audition. Each casting director may feel different in this situation, but most like to get to know the actor—even for just a brief moment—before the audition. If you arrive in character, we may not get to see you. The choice is yours. If the character you are auditioning for is a positive one, you will experience few problems. However, if the character you are auditioning for is very unpleasant, it is wise to come in as yourself and then make the transition into the character. It may not be obvious that you are in character; we may just think you are unpleasant. If being in character from the get-go helps you with your audition, do it. Be aware, though, of the impression you may leave.

GETTING PHYSICAL

From the beginning of your audition, you may have multiple occasions to physically interact with casting directors and producers. From shaking hands to bringing the casting director or reader into the scene, each has its positive and negative aspects. It is best to err on the side of caution for each case.

Shaking Hands

Shake hands with the casting director only if they extend a hand to you. A casting director will see anywhere from one to fifty actors a day (sometimes more), and may not want to shake that many nervous, clammy hands.

If you have a cold or the flu and still come in for your audition, do *not* shake the casting director's hand even if offered. Some actors will still come in if they are ill and shake the casting director's hand. The casting director gets sick, misses work, or worse, can't miss work; so comes in and gets everyone else sick. If you are sick and still want to come in, fine. But tell the casting office and don't shake anyone's hand. Everyone will appreciate it.

As for producers' sessions, the same rule applies. If producers move to shake your hand, feel free. If not, don't. (There can be ten or more people in that room and the first twenty minutes can be taken up by an actor's desire to shake each and every hand in sight.) Just say hello, be friendly and let the casting director show you where to sit or stand.

Sitting or Standing

The dilemma of sitting or standing during an audition also seems to cause a lot of confusion to actors. There is a very simple solution—ask. Most of the time the decision will be yours. If they want you to stand (or sit) but you feel like doing the opposite, it is best to do as they have requested. Their decision may be based on previous experiences during the audition process. Be cautious. If the scene is high energy (even in dramatic pieces), be very careful that you don't lose the energy if you choose to sit down. In comedy it is usually better to stand during your audition just to keep your energy up.

Physical Interaction

In order to keep their energy at the correct level, many actors will inadvertently bring the casting director into the scene in a physical way. Remember, the casting director is not an actor. Don't touch him or her during the reading. They are not in the scene with you, but are merely reading with you as the casting director evaluates your work. Some casting directors may be very animated or seem to *give more* in the reading. Others may give you absolutely nothing. Regardless, don't make them uncomfortable by bringing them into the scene.

If there is some action you find necessary to the passion of the scene—for example, hitting or kissing—either mime it or let your acting convey the sentiment through your intensity. Should you want to touch the casting director in any manner during the audition, ask before you go in the room. The worst they can do is say, "No." Otherwise, it is wise not to touch, hit, bite, abuse, kiss, tickle or otherwise torture the casting director.

SAYING THE WRONG THING

Words are powerful tools. What you say in every audition, whether it be a question or part of a conversation, is very important. An excellent audition can be hurt by impromptu words that seem harmless.

Asking Questions

Asking questions is not only acceptable, but is strongly encouraged if the questions are relevant to your character or the scene. In most auditions (including callbacks) the casting director, producer, or director will ask if you have any questions. If you've done your homework and have none, great. If you do, then ask them. If you have questions and don't ask them, you are passing up an opportunity for guidance.

There is a proper time and place for every question, however. Try to have as many of the minor questions (e.g., technical questions such as whether the role is a featured or co-star role) answered by your agent or manager before going to the audition. If they don't have the answer and you feel the questions can be answered by the casting assistant, ask him or her once you are in the office. The goal is to save only those questions absolutely necessary for the casting director.

The same goes for producers' sessions. If your questions can be answered before you go in the room, have them answered. Having a million questions for the producers (especially frivolous ones) can be time-consuming. Don't waste a producer's time. Ask your

> Once I was reading the role of a little boy being abused by his father. The scene was very emotional, resulting in the father hitting the child. Wanting to keep the intensity of the scene, the auditioning actor decided he would grab my face. It scared the hell out of me, and made me extremely wary of the actor and his control.—E. K.

NEXT!
An Actors Guide
to Auditioning

agent first, the casting assistant second, the casting director third, and the producers last.

Avoid questions about anything other than your character or the scene. Also, avoid making suggestions. Only when you get the job might it be appropriate to make suggestions. Don't do it in the audition.

"Nice To Meet You"

If you are an established actor, chances are that at some point you will bypass a preread with a casting director and go *straight-to-producers* on any number of projects. In making the decision to bring you straight in, the casting director is usually well aware of your body of work. Saying, "Nice to meet you" to a casting director in front of producers can unintentionally leave the impression that the casting director doesn't know you or your work. If you are called straight-to-producers by a casting director you have never met, simply either thank the casting director for bringing you in or say, "Nice to see you." This way you avoid any misunderstandings which may affect the producers' view of the casting director.

Reading The Script

If a script is available for a project, take the time to read it. If circumstances prevent you from reading it, mentioning that fact in a preread is generally acceptable. Avoid mentioning it in a callback, as producers may feel you are starting your audition off with an excuse or qualification of your reading. If you do mention the fact that you haven't read the script, be absolutely honest in your reasons. Stating that you didn't know a script was available or that you didn't get one (when you know you had a copy or access to one) will only serve to make the casting director look bad and you look ignorant or lazy.

Unfamiliar Television Projects

If a television series has been on the air for a considerable amount of time, there is no excuse for not seeing it at least once. However, if you have missed the show, the only time you should ever admit that you haven't seen it is in the casting director's office. Admitting this in front of the producers is not smart.

If your audition is straight-to-producers, make sure that you call the casting director with any questions about the show before your audition. They will appreciate your call, even if they are busy. They want you to do your very best and will always try to make time to answer any questions you may have.

Fishing for a Callback

Don't ask a casting director if you are going to get a callback after the preread. It puts everyone in an awkward position. In truth, the casting director probably hasn't decided that yet. It all depends on how many people the casting director will be bringing to the producers, how good your audition was, and if you are right for the project. Many decisions can be made between the time of your preread and the actual callback. If you would like a time frame as to when you should stop waiting for the phone to ring, simply ask the casting director when callbacks are scheduled. This way, you'll know when to stop wondering if you'll get one, and not force the casting director into an awkward position.

THE ART OF CONVERSATION

Some casting directors, producers or directors may want to chitchat for a minute and others may not. It all depends on the dynamics of each particular project. If someone in the room doesn't want to be chatty, don't push the issue. If they do want to talk a bit (even though you may simply want to get down to business,) you have a few options.

You can answer their questions and then, when they appear ready, ask for a moment or two before you start. Remember, a moment or two to collect yourself is just that—a moment or two. Turn around and take a deep breath. Turn back when you are ready to begin. An elaborate production isn't necessary and preparation that takes any longer should have been done before walking into the audition.

If the producers are chatty and you are not, another option is to ask politely if you may read first and answer any questions later. Most times they will not have a problem with that. (It also gives them the opportunity to see what you've come up with.) After your reading, the casting director and producers may no longer want to chat. It has nothing to do with the quality of your audition. Usually the casting director or producer is only chatting at the start of the audition in order to make the actor feel more comfortable.

After your reading, there may be an awkward moment or a complete lack of conversation. Never take the pauses which immediately follow a reading as commentary on your audition. More often than not, these pauses are simply caused by the awkwardness of how to say good-bye. The casting director usually breaks this silence and thanks you for coming in. If not, kindly thank the producers for seeing you and simply leave the room. In a callback, a producer may occasionally ask about a school you attended or a credit on your resume. Be succinct and to the point in your response and then, when the conversation is finished, thank them, and leave.

Humorous, relevant anecdotes are wonderful responses to questions, but when they become long and drawn-out stories, they can actually hurt your chances of booking a job. If you find yourself rambling on, just find a point at which you can gracefully end the story. Don't sweat it. As long as you are talented and don't take an eternity, it won't hurt you. All auditions can be nerve-wracking.

> An actor once asked me if he could have a moment to prepare and then started doing yoga for *five minutes* in front of the producer, director and writer. First, I had to ask the actor to go outside to finish his "preparation," and then I had to beg the producers to let this guy come back in. Needless to say, he did not get the job.—E. K.

PROPS

Props can hurt an audition. Usually when actors use props, they are relying more on the props than on the written word or their own talent. This is true in dramatic pieces and especially true in comedy. If you are auditioning for a comedy you must have faith that the written words are funny and that you are funny using them. If you bring a prop in, many casting directors will immediately think that you are relying on that prop for laughs. Props can also become the focus of the scene, thereby distracting your viewers from your acting.

One of the most common props brought into an audition is a cigarette. Not only is it inappropriate to light up during a reading, but in some parts of the country, it is illegal to smoke in a public building. Smoking is always distracting to the audition process. If you would like to mime simple props (e.g., talking on the telephone or smoking), feel free. Make sure that you keep your movements specific and unobtrusive to the scene. If the mimicry takes more than one second of the scene or becomes the focus of the scene, your best bet is to simply leave it to everyone's imagination. You have so many other things to worry about that bringing in props that may distract from your reading, could only hurt your chance of a successful audition. Leave the props at home.

While working on a pilot, I brought in an actor to read for the producers. The role was that of a man under a great deal of pressure. In the stage directions, the character takes an antacid. Unbeknownst to all of us watching the audition, the actor had actually brought in an antacid and began to chew on it during his reading. Something he didn't count on happening, did. The antacid changed colors and blue foam started pouring from his mouth. Not only was it disgusting to watch, it also completely pulled our focus away from the actor and his talent. —E. K.

CHANGING THE DIALOGUE

Never change a single word of dialogue. Ever.

Recently, I had an actress read for the producers who loved her interpretation. They laughed and laughed and told her, in no uncertain terms, that her audition was terrific. The actress, for some reason, was extremely dissatisfied with her performance and asked to give it another go. I reassured her that the first reading was fine, but the actress persisted. Finally, the director piped up and said, "Why don't you quit while you're ahead." She did and got the job.—E.K.

COUNTERING DISTRACTION

You've just started the scene and you suddenly notice that the casting director reminds you of your ex. Or you remember that it's your mother's birthday and you forgot to send her a card. Those thoughts can throw you off, but you keep going . . . and going . . . and going. You finish the scene and run out of the room because you know how unfocused you were. The whole trip home, you kick yourself because you did the scene perfectly twenty minutes ago in the bathroom mirror. You actually had some options.

If you find yourself becoming distracted or unfocused as you read the scene (whether you're in a preread or callback), stop yourself immediately. Ask if you may start over. Usually, the answer will be yes. If you do, make sure you are focused and capable of doing it again. However, don't decide to stop on the seventh page and ask to start from the top. The casting director might say that the reading was just fine and not to do it again. That may be true, or just a nice form of rejection—either you weren't right for the part, or you completely missed the target. Often casting directors are behind schedule and just don't have the time. Don't argue the point. You can always call your agent for specific feedback later.

Before you ask the casting director, producer or director if you can do the scene again, however, you should be aware of your state of mind. Was the audition really terrible or are you being overly hard on yourself?

If you are being hard on yourself, you are doing yourself a great disservice by asking for another crack at the scene. Many actors have actually talked themselves out of jobs by pleading to do it over—even when the scene was perfectly acceptable. Learn how to let it go. If you are having an "off" day (you can't be brilliant all the time) chalk it up to experience. You should call your agent to let them know how you felt you did. That way when the agent speaks with the casting director, the agent can let them know that you had an "off" day. It happens. Keep in mind how uncomfortable the other people are in the room if you keep asking to do the scene over and over again. Cut your losses and leave without making everyone more uncomfortable.

DIRECTION

Learning to take and understand direction is an incredible skill and one which every actor (even well-established actors) needs to continue to develop throughout their career. There will be times that you don't agree with the direction, don't understand it, or get confused by different direction from different people. Be flexible and ready to make a change at a moment's notice.

Creative Interpretation

An actor may have an interpretation of the character that is radically different from what is indicated on the written page. While a casting director does not want to stifle your creativity or tell you what your sub-text should be, they also don't want you to be so far off-the-mark that they feel you are wrong for the part. If you have a unique view of the scene, ask if the casting director would like to see it. If he advises you to stick to the more traditional approach, do just that. If the casting director wants to see your interpretation, immediately after the reading ask if there are any adjustments. If the casting director gives you direction or asks to see another version of the scene, listen carefully and make sure you understand what was said.

When my partner and I were casting a guest starring role on a series, the director gave an actor direction which was discussed in-depth. After the second reading, however, it was clear to everyone (including the actor) that he was grappling with making the adjustment. He asked to do the scene one more time and, after that reading, he still was not satisfied, but thanked everyone and headed home. We pressed on with the session, and, twenty minutes later, that actor showed up in the waiting room and said, "I got all the way home and finally understood the direction. Can I read again?" After checking with the producers, my partner and I invited him in and he read again. Not only did he "get it," he got the job.—P.B.

If your audition is straight-to-producers, and you have a different slant on the character, call the casting director beforehand. This way, if you are really going a different direction than the producers want, you will know it before your audition.

Asking for Direction

Most actors ask casting directors or producers if they would like to see the scene done another way. When asking this question, actors are very often looking for specific direction, which in most cases they will get. Be careful, though, how you ask for direction. If you ask them if they want to see it another way, occasionally the director may simply say, "Okay, do it another way." Be prepared for that.

Understanding Direction

Often, directors and producers are not clear when giving an actor direction. Don't pretend to understand and then do the scene. You might leave the director with the impression that you can't take direction. Listen carefully; if you don't understand, politely ask for clarification.

Contradictory Direction

When casting directors give you direction during or after prereads, they are passing on their interpretation of what the producers are looking for. During a callback, if you receive direction that differs from what the casting director has told you, always do what the di-

NEXT!
An Actors Guide
to Auditioning

rector or producer requests. The casting director could have an inaccurate view of the character, or the producer/director may have had a change of mind somewhere in the process.

Disagreeing with Direction

When a casting director, producer, or director gives you an adjustment, either they are telling you what they are looking for, or testing your range as an actor. You have no way of knowing what their motivation is, so do as they ask. If you don't agree with the direction, don't argue the point. Sometimes the director isn't considering this change but wants to see it done another way. Or maybe he wants to gauge how well you take direction. So grin and bear it. Wait until you are hired to discuss direction.

INSTANT CALLBACKS

After reading for a casting director, you may be sent off immediately to read for the producers. What do you do when this happens? Realize that because of production time constraints, there is a need to cast this role quickly. However, treat this instant callback just as you would any other callback. It's just happening a little faster than normal. The stakes aren't any higher than they were before you walked through the door. Use that nervous energy in your audition. It's a better outlet and easier on the stomach.

Occasionally you will come into the casting director's office for an audition and, after reading, be asked to wait in the outer office until the producers and director get there. "We're going to make a decision immediately and send you to the set" is not an uncommon phrase to hear in the casting world. This is a *group instant callback* and it is more common in television.

When you return to the outer office, there may be four or five other actors also waiting for the producers' session. When you walk out of the casting director's office, do not announce to the rest of the room that you were asked to stay for the producers, as there may be others who have not read for the casting director

When I was an actor, my second professional L.A. audition was for the feature film FOR KEEPS starring Molly Ringwald. My agent told me that I would have a general meeting with casting director Caro Jones who was looking for the lead male role opposite Ringwald. I would just chat with her; a reading was not scheduled. At the office, Jones was incredibly pleasant and the conversation enjoyable. Then she asked, "Will you read for this role of Molly Ringwald's boyfriend?"

I studied the sides in the outer office and, when I was ready, Caro welcomed me back into the office. I read. She gave adjustments. I read again. When we were done, Caro informed me that she wanted me to meet John Avildsen, the director. That was my first experience with an *instant callback*. —P.B.

yet and who may not be asked to stay. Be considerate of the other actors.

After you have all read for the producer/director, you will be asked to remain outside until released. Finally, the casting director will come out and say something like, "Well, you were all wonderful and thank you for coming in. We'd like _____ to stay." Only one name will be announced. This is the most difficult announcement for casting directors to make. They hate it, but sometimes it's necessary.

If you're not the one asked to report to work, chalk it up to experience and don't beat yourself up about it. You did your best and that's all you can do.

If you do get the job, please be considerate of the other actors. This is not an appropriate time to let out a yelp and shout, "I got it! I got it!" Also, do not report to the set (this includes makeup and wardrobe) until the casting director has talked to your agent, and you have confirmed with your agent that the deal has closed.

TROUBLESHOOTING

While many of the problems seem fairly minor and easily dealt with, others can be more difficult and more stressful. Remain calm, work through them and come up with options and solutions that work for you.

NEXT!
An Actors Guide
to Auditioning

Conflicting Work Dates

If you audition for a project which is scheduled to shoot on a date for which you have a prior work commitment, tell the casting director immediately. Before your audition your agent should have (and even may have) given the casting director this information, but it is always safe to bring it up again. Upon hearing you have a conflict, some casting directors may opt not to proceed with the reading. Others will press on with the audition in order to get to know you and your work. If the casting director is convinced that you are perfect for the role, he or she may bend over backwards to resolve work conflicts. Who knows, you may end up with two jobs running concurrently.

The Wrong Sides

Occasionally, you may show up for an audition only to be told that you were given the wrong material to prepare. Look over the new sides if they are for the same character. They may not have changed that much and you may be able to go on with the audition as planned. The essentials of the character are usually the same, the words are just different. If the changes are drastic, ask to be rescheduled and, if they are unable to do so, take the time you need to prepare. Don't be rushed but also be considerate of the casting director's schedule and take no more time than necessary.

If the new sides are for a completely different character, a casting director or assistant should offer to reschedule your appointment (if possible) for another day. Do yourself a favor and don't be a martyr. If you're offered a rescheduled time, take it. If not, request it. It is your audition and you deserve sufficient time to prepare. It may not be feasible for the casting director to reschedule, but at least you will have tried.

Questions of Age and Ethnicity

This is the most common dilemma actors can face in a casting office. What you should know is that it is illegal (by union standards as well as by Federal statute) for a casting director or producer to ask your ethnic heritage or your age. The only exception is when dealing with children under the age of 18 as social workers, studio teachers and restricted work hours then enter the need for the picture. Just because they can't ask, however, doesn't mean they won't. Be tactful when responding. Whatever you do, refrain from standing up defiantly and saying, "You're not allowed to ask that!"

When dealing with age questions, subtly let them know that they have asked an inappropriate question by offering up your *age-range*. "I've played 18 to 23" is a good way of responding. This way, you are giving them some information while not being specific. Be realistic in your age flexibility. On stage, you may be able to play 18 to 72 (with very good makeup) but on screen, your range is generally only a five year span.

What if the casting director or producer continues to push for your exact age? Only you can tell what the right thing to do is when they are relentless in their pursuit. Be firm, pleasant and not confrontational about it. When you leave the office, let your agent know what happened and consider making an anonymous complaint to your union. Chances are, the casting director or producer is not aware of union rules regarding questions of age and simply need to be informed.

Being asked your heritage is a little tougher to deal with than the age question and requires a bit more tact in handling. As with age, casting directors, producers and directors are not allowed to ask the specific heritage of "minority" actors but it is a difficult rule to enforce.

In 1986, realizing the hardships that minority performers face, a group of entertainment professionals founded the *Non-Traditional Casting Project (NTCP)*, a not-for-profit advocacy organization. The NTCP's purpose is to address and seek solutions to the problems of racism and exclusion in theatre, film and television. Thus, the term *nontraditional casting* was born.

Nontraditional casting is the casting of actors of color, actors with disabilities, and female actors in roles where race, ethnicity, physical ability or gender are not essential to the character's or play's development. The NTCP's goal is that one day actors will be cast solely on the basis of individual talent rather than how they conform to stereotypes. The NTCP has been instrumental in influencing decision-makers to hire these artists on the basis of individual merit and have helped narrow the discrimination gap existing in our industry today.

Work by the NTCP has helped to raise awareness about the true meaning of nontraditional casting. Unfortunately, there have been misunderstandings of the NTCP's work which have lead to an interesting new concept . . . *heritage-specific casting.*

Some producers have misunderstood, interpreting nontraditional casting to mean that a specific ethnic minority character should be played only by an actor of that specific heritage. (e.g., only Chinese Americans should play Chinese characters.) From most casting director's vantage point, the only time that specific cultural heritage comes into play is when the actor is required to speak a native language fluently. Even then, the question, for example, should not be, "Are you Filipino?" but "Do you speak Tagalog?" Not everyone thinks like us, unfortunately, as this is not the norm.

If you are a minority performer who is asked about your heritage, you can handle the situation in several ways.

Disarming them with humor is one of the easiest ways to worm yourself out of a difficult situation. If you're Mexican American and the role is Cuban, when asked about your heritage answer (with tongue firmly in cheek) "Scottish." Hopefully, the casting director or producer will get the message and enjoy the humor of the situation. If not, you have a difficult choice to make.

You can also humor them by giving them the answer they are looking for (commonly called "lying through your teeth.") If you decide to take this tact, be certain that there is nothing (such as the character speaking a language you do not) that could affect your on-job performance.

Another option is to be honest and risk ruling yourself out of a part. It all depends on your stance on heritage-specific casting.

Although "ignorance of the law" is no excuse, many casting directors, producers and directors are simply unaware of the union's standing on ethnic questions and merely need to be told. Let your union handle the dissemination of that information by reporting the incident to the appropriate representative. Remember, if you feel you were intentionally discriminated against because of race, sex, disability, or sexual orientation, report it to your union. They are there to support you.

Being Videotaped

With the advent of portable video cameras, videotape has become an important part of the casting process. You should be prepared to be *put on tape* if the situation arises. Usually you will know that you are going to be taped even before you walk through the door. Casting directors will inform your agent if that is going to happen so that you will be prepared. (In commercials, most auditions are put on tape. Don't expect your commercial agent to remind you each time you go on a call.) Occasionally, a casting director will not know this in advance. For example, a producer may be unavailable for the session or have flown to New York at the last minute but still wants to see the choices.

If you are surprised by videotape equipment in the room, be professional. Work with the director or casting director in figuring out the logistics of it. Do they want you to look into the camera? Do they want you to choose a spot off-camera to relate to? Do they want you to sit or stand? These are all questions you should ask. By asking what their preferences are, you are showing that you are able to work with them. You have become a team player. And everyone likes team players.

If you feel your reading was unfocused due to the videotape, ask if you may begin again. They may or may not let you. Accept their decision. You may have done much better than you thought.

Nudity

With the advent of cable programming and progressive shows like Steven Bochco's NYPD BLUE, nudity on television is quickly catching up with feature films. While the majority of nude scenes are still delegated to the female roles, more and more male actors are displaying bare bottoms (and sometimes more) on the small and silver screens. This is a personal decision for every actor regardless of gender. Only you can decide what is best for you.

First, your agent should inform you before you get to the casting director's office that the project calls for you to appear nude. You need to make the decision about whether or not you are willing to do nudity before you accept the audition. If you are not interested, pass. If you are on the fence about whether or not to do it, don't. It is extremely unprofessional to come in for a role you truly aren't interested in, and you are also putting the casting director in a bad position. If the producers want to hire you and then can't, the casting director will bear the blame.

If you are willing to do nudity, there are some things you should know about the audition process. First, you are never expected to remove your clothing in a preread with a casting director. Most casting directors will tell your agent that you should, "Wear something that shows off your body." If you are ever asked to take your clothes off, tell them that you were not informed of that requirement. Suggest that you proceed with the reading portion of the audition (or reschedule your appointment) until you have had a chance to talk with your agent.

Once you have gotten past the preread and onto the producers' session, you may be asked to doff your clothing at that point. However, your agent should be aware of that before you go in for the callback and should tell you they want to see you in . . . well, your birthday suit. Again, if you're placed in an uncomfortable position of not knowing ahead of time, ask to speak with the casting director in the outer office for a moment and phone your agent.

On those rare occasions when nudity is required during a producer's session, be sure you know exactly what is expected. You don't want to expose more than necessary. Also, confirm with your agent that there will be a minimum number of people present during the audition, no video cameras in the room, and the specifics of how this will be handled. You may request that a casting director (or assistant) of the same sex as yourself be the only individual in the room as a judge of your body. Another option which is becoming quite common is the use of a Polaroid camera which produces photos instantly and without negatives. Ask that an individual (of the same sex) take a Polaroid shot of your body which may then be shown to the producers (who should wait in the other room). Once the picture has been seen by the producers, request it back immediately. If a producer or director wants to retain the picture, you are within your rights to refuse such a request or to ask the casting director to return the photo to you at a later date.

Casting directors hate to have an actor go through this process and generally are quite sensitive to your vulnerability. In most cases they and the producers will make sure you are treated well in a potentially embarrassing situation. If, after the audition, you feel you were mistreated or exploited in any manner, do not hesitate to contact your union or law enforcement officials.

Sexual Harassment

In old Hollywood, stories of starlets being offered roles in exchange for sex were common and gave birth to the term, *casting couch*. Although awareness has helped reduce the frequency of this abuse, it would be naive to believe that the casting couch does not exist in some form in Hollywood today. You must be prepared to deal with it should it happen to you.

Sexual harassment is against the law, plain and simple. It is an abuse of power. It can take on many forms—man to woman, woman to man, man to man, woman to woman—and always feels demeaning. You must remember, you have done nothing wrong. Should you find someone offering you a job in exchange for sex or making inappropriate advances, leave the office. Again, talk to your agent and your union.

Offensive Material—Pass or Accept

This situation—mainly faced by ethnic performers and women—can involve stereotypic characterizations, religious or political statements you do not agree with, or sexual situations which you find distasteful. You do have several options when dealing with offensive material.

Pass on the initial preread if you feel uncomfortable with the role or project. If the material is so offensive that you can't fathom being able to bring dignity to the role, then tell your agent you would rather not read. Your agent can then tell the casting director that you were uncomfortable with the material and are passing on the role. Remember, many times it is very hard for us to ask anyone to perform a very stereotypical role. We will understand if you choose not to come in.

Accepting the audition is an alternative and allows you to express your concerns to the casting director. This works best when the role is salvageable in some manner or another, and you feel that you can bring some dignity to it through your interpretation. The casting director can tell you how tied the producers are to the specific stereotype and may even pass your concerns onto them after you have left the audition. (This can even be a first step in producers rethinking a stereotypic role.)

If you receive a callback for an offensive role, you must decide whether you are willing to go through with the producers' session. If, after your discussion with the casting director, you feel the producers flat out want a stereotype, then you should pass on the callback. If you feel the producers may be open to your concerns, accept the callback and, in a non-confrontational manner, bring up your concerns with the producers when you are in the room. (Be sure to have expressed these feelings to the casting director before bringing it up to the producers. Otherwise you will have a surprised and possibly very angry casting director.) Then do your reading and bring as much dignity to the role as you can. However, if you accept the callback without expressing your concerns to the producers, you had better be prepared to do the role exactly as they want it. Once you have gotten the job is not the time to decide you don't like it. Speak now or forever hold your peace.

CHANGING THE DIRECTOR'S MIND

So, what do you do if you're upset that you didn't get a callback or the feedback on your audition was not positive? How do you break the rules but remain professional? An acceptable manner of dealing with this situation is to ask your agent to get you another preread with the casting director. Many casting directors are open to seeing a performer again if they have the time. If you are unable to get another reading with the casting director, there will be other opportunities. If you do get a second reading but still don't get a callback, let it go. It was not meant to be. There's always next time.

AND THE JOB GOES TO...

After any audition, many actors go home and begin the gut-wrenching process of understanding why they didn't get the callback or the job. There are many reasons, and one of the easiest ways of finding out is to ask for *feedback*.

After every audition always ask your agent to get a brief summary of what you did right or wrong in your audition. Most casting directors give feedback, and it can be an important gauge of what you need to work on in your auditioning skills. However, be realistic. Wait at least a day or two before asking for it. It may take a few days for the casting director to gather his or her thoughts and for someone to get back to your agent. Never call the casting director yourself. It places the casting director in an awkward situation regardless of whether their comments are positive or negative. Always let your agent or manager handle it.

Most casting directors will happily pass on their thoughts about a particular audition. Others won't—they may have had a bad experience and decided to avoid possible misunderstandings that arise from misinterpretation. Others will give only generic, nonspecific feedback, not wanting to hurt an actor's feelings. Regardless, hearing any type of response will bring a feeling of closure to each audition and may even help you realize the various reasons you may not have gotten the callback or the job.

PHYSICAL TYPE
Often, an actor won't get the callback because he or she doesn't look like the character as envisioned by the producer, writer or

director. It's very easy to find the exact look you want because there are so many actors in Hollywood to choose from. Usually everyone going to the producers' sessions is capable of doing the work. It's just a matter of giving the producer choices.

STAR POWER

As the entertainment industry is a for-profit business. Television shows and movies are either developed around "names" (recognizable, bankable stars) or stars will be hired for a guest starring role in a series or co-starring role in a film. The producers want the name value to help sell the project. At some point in your career the part will be given to someone who never auditioned but has some kind of name value. With luck, one day you'll be that star and someone else will be cursing you for getting "their role."

FRIENDS AND FAMILY

You may lose a role to someone the casting director has never met. This actor may not even be able to act. Scary? Frustrating? Yes, for both you and the casting director. Move on, though—you'll never be able to compete with the producer's newest "friend," or the director's daughter, or . . .

YOUR OWN WORST ENEMY

Another way actors can lose out on a role is by talking their way out of it. (See "Countering Distraction.") When an actor starts offering ideas before booking the job, the producers may think, "Wow, if this guy's a handful in the audition, he's gonna be a handful on the set." You've just talked yourself out of being hired.

Then there are those self-deprecating actors—no matter how brilliant their reading was—verbalize their dissatisfaction with their performance to the producers. "Oh, I can do it better. That was really awful." At this point the casting director may be smiling but they're actually fighting off the desire to jump up and strangle you. Do yourself a favor, if you feel you've done less than your best, ask if they would like to give you some direction. If they see a problem, chances are they will do just that or let you do the scene again. There are enough people in that room judging you without you joining the group.

COMPETITION

There are times when an actor will walk out the door and, unbeknownst to him, have the part. The producer then sees someone else who changes their perception of the character. They find that intriguing, and the part goes to them. It's all a combination of talent, luck, timing, mood and a lot of other factors at any given moment.

Conversely, you may get a role by default. Someone else actually got the part but due to illness, vacation plans, or booking another job can't do the job—and you get the part!

As you can see, there are thousands of reasons you may or may not get the role. Anything can happen. The best thing you can do is have fun and know that if it is meant to be, you'll get the role. Sometimes you can get a job without even auditioning. The producer might remember you from an audition you did several weeks ago and decide you are right for this one. Casting directors love calling actors and offering them parts.

NEGOTIATING THE DEAL

Leave all contract negotiations to your agent or entertainment attorney, but do have a solid working knowledge of major deal points. The more familiar you are with the "business" of "show business," the better you will understand how the system works and what you are entitled to receive.

The easiest way to discuss negotiations is to review the sample *deal memo* (on the following page) line by line and describe the information in it. While the details may vary from studio to studio and production company to production company, this should give you a solid introduction to deal memos.

(please turn to the following page)

CASTING DEAL MEMO

(a) DATE:_____

(b) PROJECT:_____

(c) EPISODE TITLE:_____

(d) ROLE:_____

(e) PROD. No:_____

(f) ARTIST'S NAME:_____

(g) ADDRESS:_____

_____

(h) PHONE:_____

(i) SS No:_____

(j) CORP:_____

(k) FED I.D.:_____

(l) AGENCY:_____

(m) AGENCY PHONE: _____

(n) AGENT:_____

(o) AGENT HOME PHONE: _____

(p) AGENCY ADDRESS:_____

(q) MANAGER:_____

(r) MANAGER PHONE:_____

(s) START DATE:_____

(t) SALARY:_____

(u) GUARANTEED DAYS:_____

(v) BILLING:_____

(w) LOOPING:_____

(x) SPECIAL PROVISIONS:_____

(y) EXPENSES:_____

_____

(AA) ROUND TRIP AIRFARE:_____   (BB) HOTEL:_____

(CC) PER DIEM:_____

SAG STATUS:_____ WARDROBE:_____ SCRIPT:____ CONTRACT:_____

WORK CALL:_____ DAY PLAYER:_____ WEEKLY PLAYER:_____

REVISIONS:

SAG REPORT DATA:

Sample Casting Deal Memo

NEXT!

An Actors Guide
to Auditioning

THE DEAL MEMO

(a) *Date:* The date upon which the deal was closed.

(b) *Project:* The title of the project will appear on this line, whether it be an episodic series, MOW, mini-series or feature film.

(c) *Episode Title:* The specific title of the TV series episode for which you are being hired.

(d) *Role:* The character you are playing.

(e) *Prod. No:* The code number/episode number assigned to a specific production. Used for production company bookkeeping reasons, it is essentially an account number.

(f) *Artist's Name:* Your name exactly as you are listed with your union or guild and exactly as you would like your on-screen credit to read. This should always be checked carefully by you and your agent on all contracts and deal memos to avoid any misspellings.

(g) *Address:* Your personal home address to which any materials (including script and script revisions) can be sent. (Always keep your agent informed of any address changes.)

(h) *Phone:* Your home phone number is listed here. If there are additional numbers through which you can be reached quickly (e.g., car phone, pager, voice-mail) they should also be listed. Make sure your agent has all of your most up-to-date numbers.

(i) *Social Security No:* Your social security number for IRS and SAG work clearance purposes.

(j) *Corporation:* Some actors form a corporation for themselves for tax reasons. Essentially, instead of you being paid directly for your work, your corporation is paid for your services. The name of your corporation is listed here.

(k) *Federal Taxpayer Identification No:* The Federal Taxpayer I.D. number assigned by the U.S. Government to your corporation.

(l) *Agency:* The talent agency which represents you and has negotiated the deal.

(m) *Agency Phone:* Your talent agency's phone number.

(n) *Agent:* The particular agent at your agency who negotiated this deal on your behalf. (Can be a different agent for each job you book)

(o) *Agent Home Phone:* The home phone number of your agent.

(p) *Agency Address:* The mailing address of your talent agency.

(q) *Manager:* Your personal manager's name.

(r) *Manager Phone:* Your manager's office phone number.

(s) *Start Date:* The date upon which you will start work on the project. With a start date, there are two variables. You can be booked on a firm start date (in which case the date will read very simply February 10, 1997, for example) or you can be booked *on-or-about* a certain date. The latter situation gives production companies some leeway—allowing them to start you either on that date or within one day of that date in either direction—should locations become unavailable or specific work dates need to be rearranged. For example: If you are booked on-or-about February 10, 1997, the date indicated in line (s) will read "o/a February 10, 1997," and the production company may actually start you on February 9th, 10th, or 11th. If you are booked on an on-or-about, the deal must be closed and a contract delivered to you at least seven days prior to any on-or-about date. Otherwise, on-or-about may not be used. (There is no on-or-about option when hiring artists on a day-player contract.) Some casting directors will close all of the deal points with the agent—except for the start date. The casting director will inform the agent approximately when they will work. Technically the deal is not closed without an "on or about" or a firm start date.

(t) *Salary:* The amount you will be paid per day or week. For example, if you are hired on a daily contract, your salary will read $1,000 per day (or whatever your agent has negotiated for you) and you will be paid that amount for each day you work. If you are hired on a weekly contract, it shall read your salary per week.

Under all union agreements, there is a minimum salary you must be paid. This is referred to as *scale.* Based upon your body of work or the quote from your last job, your agents will attempt to negotiate a higher salary for you. If they are unable to negotiate more money, they will request an additional 10 percent in order to cover their commission, resulting in a salary of *"Scale + 10."* Contrary to popular belief, no union rule makes it mandatory for producers to offer or pay the additional 10 percent. It must be requested by your agent and agreed upon by the producers. While it is rare that producers paying union minimums will not offer the 10 percent, it does happen and you should be aware of that possibility.

[Note: While your salary is open to negotiation, there are other factors that may affect the overall attractiveness of your deal. The specifics below are current at press time. New SAG contracts, when ratified, may changed some of these points. Check with SAG to make sure your contract is current.—E. K. & P. B.]

Feature Films

Scale for feature films with budgets in excess of $2 million is exactly the same rate as scale for television. The *Schedule F* contract, which states that if an actor is being paid $45,000 or more for the entire project, the production company is entitled to negotiate other deal points with your agent, including free rehearsal days, free photo shoot days, free *looping (ADR)* days, waiving of overtime payments (if salary is above $47,000), free travel days, and the length of time for on-or-about dates. This does not mean that you or your agent must agree to any of these additional deal points.

Low-Budget Feature Films

SAG has developed a contract designed to benefit the independent filmmaker by allowing them to pay a lower minimum rate on films with total budgets of less than $2 million. Minimums under the *SAG low-budget agreement* are substantially lower than for feature films above $2 million. You should be clear when agreeing to perform for scale as to which contract the film falls under.

Television

In television productions, SAG has several variations which do not apply to feature films. An actor may be hired on a five-day weekly contract or on an eight-day weekly contract. This allows production companies some latitude in the number of days they must hire you in relation to the money they must spend.

If you are being hired in a guest star role in episodic television, usually there is no negotiating to be done regarding salary. The studios and networks have a set pay scale, referred to as *major role performer salary* or *top-of-show*. Producers will only vary from top-of-show for name-value performers or *recurring characters*.

The top-of-show rates may vary from show to show but may never fall below the minimums set by SAG for major role performers working five days (half-hour shows) or eight days (one-hour shows.) Per SAG edicts, anyone hired as a guest star who works more than one day must be paid at the five- or eight-day top rate, depending upon the length of the program. Many studios also set their own top of show rates for co-stars and featured players. SAG does not regulate these rates as long as they do not fall below scale. (e.g., Paramount's top-of-show for a three day co-star may be $1,500 while 20th Century Fox's may be $1,450.) If you are hired on a daily contract, your salary is more open to negotiation. If you have an impressive resume or a quote from your last job, your agent will attempt to match your quote or better it. However, that is not always possible.

(u) *Guaranteed days:* The number of days or weeks you are guaranteed to be employed (and thereby paid for). For example: if you are guaranteed two days (or weeks) on a project but end up only working one day (or week) due to no fault of your own, you will be paid for your guaranteed days even if you didn't work them all. Additionally, if you work more than your guaranteed days, for each day beyond your guarantee you shall receive your daily salary (or a prorate of your weekly salary.)

Sometimes roles get cut, productions get cancelled, and actors released before getting a chance to work. If, for some reason, this happens to you and you do not work at all on the project, you are still entitled to be paid for your guaranteed length of employment. This is known as a *pay-or-play* deal and all SAG contracts include this clause.

However, if you are verbally offered a part and it is cut within 24 hours of their offer, SAG rules that as long as the actor has not worked yet or gotten an official work call, the production company does not have to pay the actor.

(v) *Billing:* In recent years, on-screen credit has become one of the most hotly negotiated aspects of a deal due to lower salaries being paid. Billing is always open to negotiation and can make a bad financial deal an extremely attractive offer, especially if your credit is an improvement over that of your last job. Depending upon the size of the role, the project, and your career, an agent can request any of the following:

Above-The-Title Credits

On-screen credit before the name of the project appears is referred to as above-the-title credit and is reserved for major stars. Producers and studios are counting on these names and their popularity to bring audiences in to the theatres. Whether or not the credit is on a *separate card* (appearing on-screen with no other names) or *shared card* (appearing on screen at the same time as other names); *Position* (e.g., first separate card or first position on first shared card,) *size* (e.g., 50 percent of the size of the title) are also usually open to negotiation.

Main-Title Credits

Credits which follow the title of the project are main-title credits. In features these are usually reserved for additional leads and supporting players. In television, main-title credits are reserved for series regulars. The same sort of negotiation described in Above-The-Title Credits applies here as well.

Opening, Act I Credits

In one-hour series television, guest stars receive their credit following the *tease*, the main titles and commercial break, and as act one of the show begins. This is known as Opening, Act I Credits.

End-Title Credits

Credits appearing after the final scene of the project are usually those of co-stars and featured players. In films, the end-title credits are usually a *crawl* of all the crew and players who worked on the project, all listed in a particular order based on their job titles and union requirements. In some cases, actors may negotiate special end title credit to appear before the crawl.

In television, co-stars and supporting players are listed in the end-titles in one-hour shows. For half-hour shows, all actors' credits (except series regulars) are in the end-titles, including the guest stars.

(w) Looping: Negotiated looping days to cover *additional dialogue required (or replaced) (ADR)* or to fix audio problems are listed here. While under Schedule F contracts, these days may be negotiated as free days, the fees for looping may also be negotiated and included here. If no looping days are indicated but you are needed to perform such services, union guidelines state that you shall be paid a prorate of your weekly salary or

your full daily rate for eight hours of work on looping days. If you work four hours or less, your salary for these services shall be one-half of your prorated weekly salary or one-half of your daily contract rate. In any event, you shall not be paid less than SAG scale for any non-free looping days.

(x) *Special Provisions:* Any special perks or conditions of employment which are not covered in a basic union contract but have been negotiated on your behalf shall be indicated here. Some of the perks may include the following:

Dressing Room

Most projects have all performers in similar dressing facilities; however, size and style of your dressing room is open to negotiation, especially if you are of considerable name or financial value to the production.

Photo Approval:

The negotiated right of an artist to accept or reject a certain quantity of publicity photos of themselves.

Work Stop Date

A pre-negotiated date on which you are no longer required to work for the production company. This prevents your current job from conflicting with your subsequent job in the event the first production goes over schedule.

Free Video Cassette

Your agent may negotiate a free VHS-format cassette of the project for you. This cassette is usually sent to you when the film is released on video.

Paid Advertising

An industry term which refers to the deal point by which your name will appear in the credit block in certain advertisements. This credit block appears at the bottom of posters (aka one-sheets), print ads you see in newspapers and magazines, television commercials. The appearance of your name in this area must be negotiated into a contract. The name is slightly deceptive in that the artist is *not paid* for the appearance of their name. Rather, the advertising in which the artist's name appears has been paid for by the production company . . . hence, *paid ads*.

Profit Participation (points)

Most major stars get points—profit participation in addition to their salaries. Points refer to percentage points of the producers' profits (gross or net profits) derived from a film project. Some stars opt to take points instead of a salary. Bruce Willis reportedly did this on LOOK WHO'S TALKING and reportedly made $25 million. Not all salary/points exchanges are this successful. While trading high salaries for points may seem a very wise move, creative bookkeeping and the success of a film can either make you very rich or leave you empty handed. Hundreds of other actors on different projects have made nothing by taking points.

Wardrobe Fees

While the unions do set minimum wardrobe fees for providing your own wardrobe, that fee is open to negotiation (albeit, usually for major stars.)

(y) Expenses: Any expenses to be paid by a production company should be listed in the appropriate spaces. Some of the more common ones follow:

Round Trip Airfare

If you are required to fly to location, the production company must provide round trip, First-Class airfare (if First Class seats exist on flights to your destination) for one individual. This is a SAG rule. An actor always has the right to waive First Class airfare in order to receive other perks. An actor who is hired and must travel to Hawaii may request two Economy Class, or Coach, tickets in order to bring along a companion.

Additionally, the producing company must allow for *travel days* (one day on each side of your flight.) Unless payment was negotiated in your contract, you are generally not paid for travel days. You will also never be asked to report to work on the same day you have traveled to a location.

Hotel

While out of town, an actor must be provided with lodging at the production company's expense—again, according to SAG's rules. The style of hotel is open to negotiation, although most actors on location stay in the same facility. One can always choose to waive provided accommodations. If an actor has a friend that lives in the location area, they may choose to stay with that friend and request that the money to be spent on their hotel be paid to them instead.

Per Diem

The amount you will be paid each day that you are required to be out of town, including travel days. Open to negotiation, this fee is meant to cover any meals or personal expenses and may never fall below the minimum *per diem* rates set by the union.

The remaining spaces on the deal memo are essentially for production company use only. Here, casting directors or production managers indicate your SAG status (if the union tells the casting office that you are *Station 12,* you have not paid your dues and are not permitted to work until you have paid them); that wardrobe has been given your contact information; that a script has been sent to you; that a contract has been typed; the time of your *work call* and to whom it has been given; whether you are a *day player* or *weekly player*; that *script revisions* have been sent to you; and which *SAG report categories* you fall under for fairness-of-employment tracking.

[Note: During your career, undoubtedly you will go through many different negotiations that we can't possibly cover in this book. If you ever have any questions regarding points of contention in any contract, consult your agent, manager, lawyer or union representative. While we have covered some of the basics here, we do not know all the guild rules as thoroughly as does your union representative. We have provided this brief summary for example purposes only, and you should check the validity of the information listed here with your applicable union.—E. K. & P. B.]

WORKING

Once you have been hired, the fun begins. You get to use your skills, make some money, and meet new and interesting people. Expect long hours, good times, frustrating times, people with great personalities, people with difficult personalities, and behavior that's both professional and unprofessional.

WHAT IS EXPECTED OF YOU

Once you've gotten on the set, remember that you have been hired to do a certain job. Regardless of how pleasant or unpleasant your experience on a set, keep in mind that you are an employee. Have fun, but remember what is expected of you.

You are expected to be punctual, whether it is simply for a *makeup call*, rehearsal or on-camera work. If you are going to shoot some scenes, then memorize your dialogue and be completely prepared. Be clean and sober and have a pleasant disposition. In other words, be a team player and be professional.

For any job, even if it is a rehearsal or *table reading* (the first full reading of a script), it is best to always be at performance level. This does not mean that what you are doing is etched in stone. You will be directed and, hopefully, have opportunities to express your ideas with the director. This is especially important to remember when working on a sitcom in a non-regular role. You will be joining an existing cast which may, at times, seem to be walking through it without doing any acting. These folks do this week in and week out and are practically family. The producers know

An actress auditioned several times for a sitcom pilot I was casting. She tested at the network and got the job. At the table read, however, the actress' performance was nowhere near as good as it was during the auditions. In a private note session with the producers following the reading, the network decided that she didn't have the "edge" for this character and replaced her.

For some reason, this actress chose not to give 100 percent at this table reading, and she lost her job. Don't make the same mistake she did.—E. K.

P.S. Don't feel too sorry for her. She currently is displaying her "edge" as one of the hottest vixens on primetime soaps today.

what they will get from their series regulars on tape night; they do not necessarily know what they will get from you. Therefore, it is very important to give it your all from the very beginning. Don't give the producers anything to get nervous about and consider replacing you.

While on the set you will have creative exchanges with everyone from the producer to the costumer. If you don't agree with a certain decision made by a crew member, it's okay to say so. In most situations, the director and the actors come to mutual understandings about what works and what does not. In some cases, arguments may ensue. However, most of the time the director (in films) or the producer (in television) is the one guiding the production and always has the final word.

ON-SET BEHAVIOR

While on the set, respect is rule number one. Each person who is working on the project, from the caterer to the producer, deserves to be working in a pleasant environment. If this isn't the case, maintain your professional demeanor at all times. Disagreements are meant to be creative, not combative, and problems are always fixable if approached in the correct manner. No matter what, temper tantrums are never justified and can haunt you later in your career.

If you are having problems with someone on the set, try to work it out with that person. Whining about it to someone else doesn't help the situation, and often makes matters worse. If it still isn't resolved, discuss the problem with the director, producer, or production manager and see what happens. Any conflicts you have should be approached in the manner that reduces your stress. Call your agents and let them handle it.

Don't talk about salaries. Not only is it impolite, but it also opens the door for hurt feelings and arguments. Unless all salaries are on a *favored nations* basis (i.e., everyone is receiving the same salary), some people on the shoot may be making more or less than you. As we all know, conversations about money can be inflammatory.

BEING REPLACED

One would think that having the job and being on the set means that you'll be there until your job is done. However, there is always a chance of being replaced.

If you are unprofessional in your approach to a job, or not doing a satisfactory job, chances are you will be replaced. There are times, however, when being replaced has absolutely nothing to do with you or your amount of talent. Creative visions can change before, during and long after you've reported to the set. There is nothing you can do to affect that.

Replacing an actor is probably the most gut-wrenching process for a casting director to go through. If you are ever replaced on a project, ask your agent if they know why rather than making yourself crazy. Chances are, unless there were major problems on the set, it has absolutely nothing to do with you.

"AND I'D LIKE TO THANK . . ."

After every audition (and once you have booked a job) your work is not finished. A very important part of developing your career is remembering to say "thank you" to all those involved. Not only is this a very good habit to develop, but following up in this way also helps to keep you in the casting director, producer or director's mind. There are various ways to keep in touch and, while the U.S. Postal Service is the easiest, the choice is yours.

THANK YOU NOTES
Thank you notes are a terrific way of saying thanks to a casting director for whom you have auditioned or a producer/director with whom you have worked. As your picture or resume is not on these cards, they convey to the recipient a feeling of genuine appreciation. It's another way to keep your name in front of the casting director, producer or director who can think of you for other projects.

POSTCARDS
Postcards with your picture and contact number on them are a wise and economical way to keep in touch. They can also act as helpful reminders or as quick publicity if you are in a play, movie or television show you would like the individual to see. Postcards are also handy to let people know that you have changed representation. Keep some pre-stamped postcards with you at all times so that you can send one off at a moment's notice.

Postcards also make nice holiday greeting cards. With so many versatile computer programs around, you can try creating one with a simple holiday theme. (If you don't have a computer, go to your local copy shop and ask for help. Kinko's, for example, has a complete computer department with several graphics programs.)

As with headshots, anything that makes your postcard clever or eye-catching (without going overboard) will help keep it on the person's desk rather than go straight into the wastebasket. Send them out only when you have something to announce or if it has been a while since you have seen the individual; not one every week. If you send them out too often their effectiveness is greatly reduced.

PICTURE AND RESUME MAILING

Many actors send out their photograph and resume almost every week. While this may seem a smart, albeit expensive, way to keep in touch, it does get annoying when you suddenly have 52 pictures of the same person coming across your desk. If you do choose to mail your picture and resume, do so with discretion. Once every couple of months feel free to send casting directors your photo and resume, especially if you have changed representation. Any more frequently than that is not necessary and can quickly drain your pocketbook.

Don't get cute when sending out your photographs and resumes. Sending any food item (e.g., candies, lollipops, and those sugar stick tubes) is not a good idea. It may seem fun, but do you really think the recipients are going to eat anything sent through the mail from someone they don't know. Save your money. Also, putting confetti or cutout foil stars into your envelope always makes an incredible mess in the casting director's office. Most mail is not opened gingerly but employing the "rip & tear" method. Confetti all over the place is not a great way to start the day.

VIDEOTAPES

Don't blindly send your video/demo reel to a casting director as it is usually counterproductive. Most casting directors prefer to read an actor for a specific role rather than watch a performance on video. The casting director will have a fuller understanding if an actor is right for a particular character. When a preread isn't possible, however, a requested tape is a good second.

If you do want to send your tape to a casting director just so they can get to know who you are, always call the office first and ask permission. It may not be convenient and you may be asked to check back with in a month or so. Calling is also smart because, if the casting director doesn't have the time to watch your tape now, they still hear your name and will hear it again when you call back in a month or so.

When you do send in your tape, don't send in your only copy. Make sure it is of broadcast quality, and is clearly marked with your name and contact number. Also make sure that when the office calls you to pick up the tape, do so promptly.

FAXES

Faxes are a fast and cheap way to keep in contact with anyone, including casting directors, directors or producers, but use them sparingly. One page thank you's, greetings, invitations or announcements are generally welcomed via fax as long as you aren't faxing every other day. The only unappreciated fax is a headshot, especially if your fax machine has a photo mode. If your fax has no such mode, the quality of your picture at the receiving end will be very bad anyway; if you do have halftone capability, faxing your photo ties up the receiving fax line far too long. Only fax your headshot if you are requested to do so.

PHONE CALLS

Because of the sheer number of phone calls a casting director, producer or director receives, phoning the office is one of the least

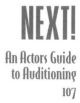

While on the phone with a producer of a film my partner and I were casting, an actor phoned the office. I politely but firmly indicated to the actor that he was calling at a bad time and asked him to call back later. The actor acknowledged what was said and hung up. Not more than 30 seconds later the same actor called back to ask when would be a good time to call. I then became angry and was dismissive. My conversation with the producer (who was unhappy with the constant interruptions) was interrupted for a third time when the same actor called back to complain about how he was treated during the previous phone call. Little wonder that I lost any good humor left in me. From the first call, the actor heard what was said but chose not to listen. Even worse, he didn't use his common sense and was not sensitive to my problems. When calling a casting office, always keep all phone calls as brief as possible and take care to really listen to what the other person is saying.

—P.B.

preferred methods for actors to keep in touch. This also applies to producers and writers you have worked with, unless you have developed a more personal relationship with them while on the set.

If you do choose to make contact by phone, keep it short. You may certainly call to say a quick hello, inform the office of changes in representation, or invite them to a play or showcase but remember how fast things move in the office. Follow up with something containing the same information through the mail or fax machine. Make sure you listen very carefully when calling the casting office.

DROPPING BY

Unless you are good friends with the person you are visiting or you know it to be a particularly slow time, dropping by is seldom advisable. If you do want to stop by and drop off a note or picture and resume, gauge how busy the office is before deciding to try and chat. If it is a busy time (which is most of the time), simply leave what you brought. You may catch the office in a lull, however, and find that the casting director has time to be social. Don't take it personally, if they don't.

No matter how you choose to follow up meetings and jobs, remember to use ingenuity, common sense, wit, grace, and finesse.

NEXT!

An Actors Guide
to Auditioning

YOUR TEAM & HOW TO FIND THEM

If you are new to the industry, you first must have your basic tools necessary, your photo and resume, to help you to assemble the team you want to have working for you. If you've been in the business a number of years and are looking to change representation, your demo reel will help make the process even easier. But what type of representation do you need? Just an agent? Or should you have a personal manager and publicist as well? The first step is to determine whom you need on your team.

TALENT AGENTS

Talent agents are the key to a successful career. Legitimate talent agents are franchised by actors' unions and have stringent rules to which they must adhere. Your agent will submit your photograph and resume for appropriate union projects, negotiate all offers, and be a guiding force in your career. Franchised talent agents are not permitted to represent nonunion talent or to negotiate nonunion contracts for their union clients. They are not allowed to charge you for sending out your picture, typing your resume, or obtaining meetings for you. A legitimate talent agency will also not charge any type of upfront fees for their services but is entitled to 10 percent of your earnings for contracts they have negotiated on your behalf.

MANAGERS

Management companies were initially formed in Hollywood's Golden Age when major stars needed someone to keep their professional lives in order. Managers read scripts for the actors and advised them as to which projects were good career moves and what amount of money was enough for their services. When the studio star system ended, the role of personal managers changed dramatically. For the most part, personal managers have basically become an extension of your agent. They submit your photograph and resume and try to get you through the casting director's door. What a manager cannot do legally is negotiate a contract on your behalf. The most they can do in that area is consult with your agent on what is acceptable money, credit, or other perks and what is not. While this is the rule of thumb, there are many managers who do negotiate contracts although the unions frown upon the practice.

Personal managers often have developed strong relationships with industry professionals, something that most agents have not done. Some managers occasionally also produce theatre, television, or feature films and, therefore, have more influence over decision makers. Additionally, managers often have fewer clients and, therefore, more time to devote to each actor's career.

Personal managers are not governed by the rules and regulations of any actor's union and therefore have more flexibility in their business practices. Managers may negotiate with you as to what percentage of your salaries they will be paid. While the typical commission charged by managers is 15 percent some managers have been known to go as low as 5 percent and as high as 20 to 25 percent.

Most personal managers do not charge actors any upfront fees. Some may ask for a small monthly fee to cover postage costs. While this is not the preferred method of operation of the *Conference of Personal Managers*, it does happen. You should think carefully before making a decision to sign with a manager who charges such a fee.

PUBLICISTS

Most actors need a personal publicist on their team only if they are currently a regular in a television series, in a major motion picture, or of significant star status. A publicist's job is to keep your face in the public eye by arranging print and television interviews or personal appearances—in other words, change you from a working actor into a celebrity.

The power of a publicist can not be understated. With the right timing and a good publicist you can be catapulted into "overnight stardom." Timing is essential. You don't need a publicist for guest starring roles on episodic television or small roles in feature films or MOW's. When you do need a publicist is when you are booked on a high profile project that can make your career. If you're in a movie with Mel Gibson but you only have two lines, save your money. However, if you're co-starring with Mel, it may be time to consider spending the money.

Publicists' fees can seem expensive, anywhere from $1,000 to $3,000 per month or higher. Sounds pricey, but it may be worth it in the long run. Buying a single full-page ad in both trade papers for one day can cost more than this.

If funds are short when you end up in a high-profile project, get to know the show's unit publicist. They are responsible for making sure that the film or television show gets good press coverage, including arranging interviews with the director, studio executives, and actors. Once the publicist has a chance to get to know you a little you may find that they will add your name to press releases and interview rosters. Essentially getting a publicist on your side without incurring any costs. The one drawback is that he or she does not become your personal publicist, and the effort will not be focused solely on you and your work. But with luck and a few pieces of press, you may experience an increase of interest from the press, and reach a point where you can eventually afford you own publicist.

The first step in securing representation is knowing what you are looking for. In theatre book stores there are many guides that can fill you in on agents, personal mangers and even publicists. Take a look at these books (we have listed some in the Suggested Reading section) as they can help you decide where to start. The books list the level of talent represented by a certain company; whether they are open to new clients or beginners; if they handle actors commercially or theatrically; and what is required to land an interview with them. Be realistic as you decide which agencies or managers to approach. If you are new to the industry, it is wise not to target talent agencies as big as The William Morris Agency, ICM, United Talent Agency or Creative Artists Agency.

Once you decide on those representatives you would like to meet, the various ways to get a meeting are basically the same for both managers and agents. Publicists are best obtained by talking with friends or other professionals who have used one.

It may seem like a long-shot, but sending your picture, resume and demo reel (if you have one) to an agent or manager who is unfamiliar with your work can actually land you representation. Choose the particular individual you want to contact at the company and write them a personalized note stating you are seeking representation. A few days or a week later you may follow up with a phone call. If they happen to have seen, remembered or loved your picture, they may agree to a meeting. After you meet, if they are interested in working with you, they may ask you to perform a prepared scene (usually if you have no demo reel) and then set up meetings with the rest of the agents/managers in the company. After this, they will decide whether to represent you or not.

Cold-Reading Workshop

Another method of landing an agent is to enroll in an industry cold-reading workshop. This is particularly helpful if you are a newcomer. These workshops pay talent agents (and casting directors) a fee to teach classes in audition techniques. An agent or casting director will give you a scene to read with another actor in front of the class. The person teaching the workshop will then give you direction and let you do the scene again. Some will give you tips on auditioning or acting. Some will just watch you do the scene and say "thank you." You should get something out of the class. Make sure you investigate the workshop. Ask other actors who have taken the class what their experiences were. Often actors land agents and even jobs this way. These classes are not free to actors. There is a fee to attend which can be relatively expensive. If you choose to go this route, look for workshops where you are required to audition before they accept you. Workshops that simply accept you if you write a check are very often avoided by agents, managers and casting directors as the quality of the actors may not be acceptable to them. Most casting directors and talent agents aren't there simply to supplement their income but to find quality people with whom to work.

It also pays to shop around for affordable showcases. Most workshops charge approximately $25—$35 per class and offer discounts for enrolling in multiple sessions or series of classes. However, some classes do charge as much as $50 to $100. Expensive is not always better.

Theatre/Film Invitation

If you are appearing in a quality play or your latest film project is airing on TV or screening locally, send out invitations/notices to every agent and manager in town. Make sure you put your contact number on the notice so if they do see your work and want to meet with you, they know where to find you.

Friend Referral

If you have a friend who is with an agent you would like to be with, ask if they will set up a meeting for you. If they agree to set up a meeting, perhaps the agents will be impressed with you and, based upon their respect for their client's judgment, will agree to represent you.

Industry Referral

If an individual you have worked with in the industry (writer, director, director of photography, casting director, casting associate) is aware that you are looking for representation, perhaps they can help you. Approach this very carefully, though. You don't want to jeopardize your relationship by being pushy or expecting too much. Make them aware of your search, and if they're willing to help, they will offer.

Once you have scheduled a meeting with potential representatives, do some investigating. Go to your union and ask to see the agency's client list (all talent agencies are required to file a client list with the Screen Actors Guild). Then remember that, when you are in the meeting, you should be interviewing them just as much as they are interviewing you. You are their partner, if the two of you choose to work together. You must be happy. You may not be putting money in their pockets right now, but you will be in the future and you deserve good work for your money.

UNIONS & GUILDS

AEA
Actors Equity Association
(Covers live theatre jobs.)

<u>Chicago</u>
203 North Wabash Avenue
Chicago, IL 60601
312/641-0393

<u>Los Angeles</u>
6430 Sunset Boulevard
Suite 700
Los Angeles, CA 90028
213/462-2334

<u>New York</u>
165 West 46th Street
New York, NY 10036
212/869-8530

<u>San Francisco</u>
235 Pine Street, Suite 1000
San Francisco, CA 94104
415/391-3838

AFTRA
American Federation of Television and Radio Artists
(Covers all radio and recording jobs some television—mostly soap operas and some prime time episodic, depending on the producing studio.)

<u>Chicago</u>
307 North Michigan Avenue
Chicago, IL 60601
312/372-8081

<u>Los Angeles</u>
6922 Hollywood Boulevard
Suite 800
Los Angeles, CA 90028
213/461-8111

<u>New York</u>
260 Madison Avenue
New York, NY 10016
212/532-0800

AFTRA—cont'd.

San Francisco
235 Pine Street
Suite 1000
San Francisco, CA 94104
415/391-7510

Seattle
601 Valley Street
Seattle, WA 98109
206/282-2596

AGVA
American Guild of
Variety Artists
(Covers all cabaret and non-
broadcast variety shows.)

Los Angeles
4741 Laurel Canyon Boulevard
Suite 208
North Hollywood, CA 91607
818/508-9984

New York
184 Fifth Avenue
New York, NY 10010
212/675-1003

SAG
Screen Actors Guild
(Covers all television and feature
film jobs.)

Chicago
75 East Wacker Drive—14th Fl.
Chicago, IL 60601
312/372-8081

Los Angeles
National Headquarters
5757 Wilshire Boulevard
Los Angeles, CA 90036
213/954-1600

New York
1515 Broadway—44th Floor
New York, NY 10036
212/944-1030

San Francisco
235 Pine Street—Suite 1000
San Francisco, CA 94104
415/391-7510

Seattle
601 Valley Street
Seattle, WA 98109
206/282-2506

(Note: For SAG offices in Arizona, Atlanta, Boston, Cleveland, Dallas, Denver,
Florida, Hawaii, Houston, Minneapolis/St. Paul, Nashville, Philadelphia, St. Louis,
San Diego and Washington D.C., call 1-800-FILMBKS to have a free listing sent
to you, or call SAG's National Headquarters at 213/954-1600.)

SUGGESTED READING

DIRECTORIES

The Academy Players Directory

National publication of professional actors. Published three times a year in four volumes by the Academy of Motion Picture Arts and Sciences. The 8.5" x 11" glossy format includes actor's photo and up to three representation contact numbers. Available for a fee to casting directors, executives and directors. (Actors are charged for their listings. Contact: The Academy of Motion Picture Arts and Sciences, 8949 Wilshire Blvd., Beverly Hills, CA 90211, 310/247-3000)

The Agency Guide

Compiled and edited by Breakdown Services, Ltd. Printed biannually and updated monthly. A comprehensive listing of Los Angeles-based talent agencies. Includes addresses, phone and fax numbers, and office personnel. (Available at theatre bookstores or through Breakdown Services, Ltd., 1120 South Robertson Blvd., Third Floor, Los Angeles, CA 90035, 310/276-9166)

The Asian American Players Guide

National compendium of Asian and Pacific Islander American talent. Published annually in June by ICMIM Productions. The 6 x 9 glossy format includes actor's photo and up to three representation contact numbers. Includes magazine style interviews and Q & A features. Distributed gratis to casting directors and at a discount to producers, executives and writers. (Actors are charged for their listings. Available through ICMIM Productions, 11684 Ventura Blvd., Suite 424, Studio City, CA 91604, 818/508-9264)

The CD Directory

Compiled and edited by Breakdown Services, Ltd. Printed four times a year. A comprehensive listing of Los Angeles-based casting directors. Includes addresses, phone and fax numbers, and office personnel. (Available at theatre bookstores or through Breakdown Services, Ltd., 1120 South Robertson Blvd., Third Floor, Los Angeles, CA 90035, 310/276-9166)

Film Actors Guide (current edition)

Compiled and edited by Steve LuKanic. Published annually in book form. Contains credits and contacts for over 5,800 working actors and actresses. Over 800 pages with several cross-indices. No charge for any listings. Also available as part of Eagle i (online service and CD-ROM.) Available from Lone Eagle Publishing Co., 2337 Roscomare Road, Suite Nine, Los Angeles, CA 90077-1851, 310/471-8066.)

Film Directors: A Complete Guide (current edition)

Compiled and edited by Michael Singer. Published annually in book form since 1982. Contains credits and contacts for over 5,000 working directors, both domestic and international, film and television movies. Over 800 pages with several cross-indices. A great resource for actors when interviewing with a director. Also available as part of Eagle i (online service and CD-ROM.) Available from Lone Eagle Publishing Co., 2337 Roscomare Road, Suite Nine, Los Angeles, CA 90077-1851, 310/471-8066.)

Film Producers, Studios, Agents & Casting Directors Guide (current edition)

Compiled and edited by David Kipen. Published annually in book form. There are four separate sections containing credit and contact information for producers; studio rosters; agency listings with personnel lists; and casting directors information with credits. All listings are free. Also available as part of Eagle i (online service and CD-ROM.) Available from Lone Eagle Publishing Co., 2337 Roscomare Road, Suite Nine, Los Angeles, CA 90077-1851, 310/471-8066.)

HOLA Directory

Directory of Latino American actors published annually by the Hispanic Organization of Latin Actors. Includes photo and representation contacts. Available to casting directors, producers, writers, executives and individuals for a fee. (Charge to actors for listing. Contact: Hispanic Organization of Latin Actors, 250 West 56th St., New York, NY 10023, 212/595-8286)

NTCP Artist Files

Located in the offices of the Non-Traditional Casting Project in New York City, the Artist Files contain the photos and resumes of over 4000 ethnic, female and disabled actors, directors, writers, designers, choreographers, stage managers, technicians, and administrators. Usage by appointment and free-of-charge. (No charge for listings. Contact: The Non-Traditional Casting Project, 1560 Broadway, Suite 1600, New York, NY 10036, 212-730-4750 or TDD: 212-730-4913)

Television Directors Guide (current edition)

Compiled and edited by Lynne Naylor. Published annually in book form since 1988. Contains credits and contacts for thousands of working directors of television series (drama and comedy), variety specials, and movies of the week. Several cross-indices are included. A great resource for actors when interviewing with a television director. Also available as part of Eagle i (online service and CD-ROM.) Available from Lone Eagle Publishing Co., 2337 Roscomare Road, Suite Nine, Los Angeles, CA 90077-1851, 310/471-8066.)

The Agencies

Updated regularly, includes detailed information on commercial, theatrical and print talent agencies, including personnel and client levels represented. *Acting World Books.*

ONLINE SERVICES & CD-ROM

Eagle i (online and CD-ROM)

All Lone Eagle's annual credit and contact directories have been combined in an enormous, relational database. All listings are free. Users can search quickly to find information on just about any major person in the entertainment industry. Hyperlinked. "Works with" function allows users instantly to compile a list of people someone has worked with. Especially useful when going in on a job interview, or trying to find the right "connection" to a pro-spective employer. (Lone Eagle Publishing Company, http://www.loneeagle.com, or call 1/800-FILMBKS.)

NTCP Artist Files Online

A computerized version of the Non-Traditional Casting Project's Artist Files. High resolution photographs of the photos and resumes of over 4000 ethnic, female and disabled actors, directors, writers, designers, choreographers, stage managers, technicians, and administrators. Transmitted via telephone lines for viewing on computer screens. (For online address, contact: The Non-Traditional Casting Project, 1560 Broadway, Suite 1600, New York, NY 10036, 212/730-4750 or TDD: 212/730-4913.)

TRADE PAPERS

Backstage

Geared towards actors and published in New York. Includes casting notices, interviews, advice columns and reviews. Published weekly in a newsprint format.

Backstage West

Los Angeles version of highly successful New York actors news source. Published weekly in a newsprint format.

Daily Variety/Variety

Published five days a week with special editions. Covers all aspects of entertainment industry news. Glossy newspaper format.

DramaLogue

Geared towards actors and published in Los Angeles. Includes interviews, casting notices, reviews and advice columns. Glossy newsprint format.

The Hollywood Reporter

Daily publication with weekend special editions. All aspects of the entertainment industry from studio deals to production charts. Glossy magazine format.

TRADE BOOKS

Acting As A Business: Strategies for Success by Brian O'Neil. A look at the "business" as a business and at the actor as businessperson. (*Heinemann;* 1993, 116 pages.)

Acting for Film & TV by Leslie Abbott. Includes basics for acting on camera. (*Star Publishing;* 1993, 296 pages with index.)

Acting for the Camera by Tony Barr. A treatise on successful on-camera acting techniques. (*Harper Publishing;* 1982, 310 pages with index.)

Acting: The First 6 Lessons by Richard Boleslavski. An enlightening discussion of the art of acting. (*Theatre Arts Books;* 1994 (38th printing, 134 pages.)

An Actor Succeeds by Terence Hines and Suzanne Vaughan: Interviews with casting directors shed important light on what helps and what hurts when trying to establish a career in Hollywood. (*Samuel French Trade.*)

The Actor's Audition by David Black. Common sense approaches to successful auditions. *(Vintage Press. 1990, 107 pages.)*

The Actor: A Practical Guide to a Professional Career by Eve Brandstein. Tips on creating a successful and professional career with class and integrity. *(Fine Publishing 1987, 289 pages.)*

The Audition Book by Ed Hooks. Brings perspective and sanity to your view of what can sometime be an insane business. *(Back Stage Books 1989, 165 pages.)*

Audition; Everything an Actor Needs to Know to Get the Part by Michael Shurtleff. The book that inspired and educated thousands of actors on the art of auditioning for stage, film and television. *(Bantam; 1978, 264 pages.)*

Film and Television Acting by Ian Bernard. Analyzes the differences between theatre, film and television acting. *(Focal Press; 1993, 135 pages with index.)*

The Glam Scam: Successfully Avoiding the Casting Couch and Other Talent & Modeling Scams by Erik Joseph. An expose of common and uncommon scams perpetrated upon aspiring actors and actresses. *(Lone Eagle Publishing; 1994, 200 pages.)*

The Hollywood Job Hunter's Survival Guide by Hugh Taylor. An insider's winning strategies for getting that all-important first job and keeping it. Expert advice from an experienced development executive. *(Lone Eagle Publishing; 1995, 314 pages with illustrations.)*

How to Audition by Gordon Hunt. Insight and advice from one of the industry's brightest directors. *(Harper & Row; 1977, 332 pages.)*

How to Audition for Movies and TV by Renee Harmon. In depth look at techniques for successful auditions, callbacks and booking the job. *(Walker Publishing Company; 1992, 238 pages.)*

How To Make It in Hollywood by Linda Buzzell. Breaking into Hollywood and smart career moves to make sure you stay in. *(Harper Press; 1992, 369 pages.)*

How to Sell Yourself as an Actor, 2nd Edition by K Callan. How to deal with the frustration of knowing your craft but not knowing the business of show business. *(Sweden Press; 1992, 240 pages.)*

The Los Angeles Agent Book, 5th Edition by K Callan. The respected actress tells you everything you wanted to know about Los Angeles Talent Agencies. *(Sweden Press; 255 pages with index.)*

The New York Agent Book, 3rd Edition by K Callan. The author does for New York agents what she did so well for Los Angeles Talent Agencies. *(Sweden Press; 265 pages with index.)*

Respect for Acting by Uta Hagen (with Haskel Frankel.) One of the bibles of acting, written with love and understanding for the art. *(MacMillan Publishing; 1973, 227 pages.)*

Screen Acting: How to Succeed in Motion Pictures and Television by Brian Adams. An in-depth discussion of techniques to market yourself, your talent and to develop your on-screen persona. *(Lone Eagle Publishing; 1987, 378 pages.)*

The Secrets To Auditioning for Commercials by Iris Acker. Includes tips for auditions and necessary skills for booking commercials. *(DP Press; 1991, 123 pages.)*

The Video Demo Tape: How to Save Money Making a Tape that Gets You Work by Larry Benedict and Suzanne Benedict. Step-by-step ways to create successful and affordable demo reels. *(Focal Press; 1992, 220 pages.)*

Word of Mouth, 2nd Edition: A Guide to Commercial Voice-Over Excellence by Susan Blu and Molly Ann Mullin. Tips for creating a successful commercial voice-over career. *(Pomegranate Press; 1992, 182 pages.)*

The Working Actor's Guide (annual) by Karin Mani: 616 pages. One of the most popular, in-depth source books for the working actor. *Mani Flattery*

Working In Commercials: A Complete Sourcebook for the Adult and Child Actor by Elaine Keller Beardsley. A guide to on-camera and voice-over commercials, industrials and print techniques for actors. *(Focal Press; 1993, 194 pages.)*

Your Film Acting Career, 3rd Edition by M.K. Lewis & Rosemary K. Lewis. Hundreds of questions about every aspect of the industry—from unions to living in Los Angeles—are answered with candor. *(Gorham House, 1993, 320 pages.)*

NETWORKS, CABLE & PRODUCTION COMPANIES

ABC (American Broadcasting Company)
2040 Avenue of the Stars
5th Floor
Los Angeles, California 90067
310/557-7777

77 West 66th Street
New York, New York 10023
212/456-7777

AMERICA IS TALKING
2200 Fletcher Ave., 6th Floor
Fort Lee, NJ 07024
201/346-6777

AMERICAN MOVIE CLASSICS (AMC)
150 Crossways Park, West
Woodbury, NY 11797
516/364-2222

ARTS & ENTERTAINMENT NETWORK
235 East 45th Street
New York, New York 10017
212/661-4500

BET (Black Entertainment Network)
1232 31st Street NW
Washington, DC 20007
202/636-2400

BRAVO CABLE NETWORK
2450 Broadway, #500
Santa Monica, California 90404
310/828-7005

150 Crossways Park West
Woodbury, New York 11797
516/364-2222

THE CARTOON NETWORK
1050 Techwood Dr., NW
P.O. Box 105264
Atlanta, Georgia 30318
404/885-2263

CBS (Columbia Broadcasting System)
7800 Beverly Boulevard
Los Angeles, California 90036
213/852-2345

NEXT!
An Actors Guide
to Auditioning

CBS—cont'd.
51 West 52nd Street
New York, New York 10019
212/975-4321

CINEMAX
HBO Building
1100 Avenue of the Americas
New York, NY 10036
212/512-1000

COMEDY CENTRAL
1775 Broadway
New York, NY 10019
212/767-8600

THE DISCOVERY CHANNEL
7700 Wisconsin Ave.
Bethesda, MD 20814
310/986-0444

THE DISNEY CHANNEL
3800 West Alameda
Burbank, CA 91505
818/569-7500

E! ENTERTAINMENT TELEVISION
5670 Wilshire Blvd.
Los Angeles, CA 90036
213/954-2400

FBC
(Fox Broadcasting Company)
10201 West Pico Boulevard
Los Angeles, California 90035
310/277-2211

40 West 57th Street
New York, New York 10019
212/977-5500

F/X
10201 West Pico Blvd., #761
Los Angeles, CA 90035
310/277-2211

THE FAMILY CHANNEL
1000 Centerville Turnpike
Virginia Beach, VA 23463
804/523-7301

HBO (Home Box Office)
2040 Century Park East
Suite 4100
Los Angeles, California 90067
310/201-9300

1100 Avenue of the Americas
New York, New York 10036
212/512-1000

HOME SHOPPING NETWORK, INC.
11831 30th Court North
St. Petersburg, FL 33716
813/572-8585

THE LEARNING CHANNEL
7700 Wisconsin Ave.
Bethesda, MD 20814
301/986-1999

LIFETIME TELEVISION
2049 Century Park East
Suite 840
Los Angeles, CA 90067
310/556-7500

36-12 35th Avenue
Astoria, NY 11106
718/482-4000

THE MOVIE CHANNEL
10 Universal City Plaza, 31st Floor
Universal City, California 91608
818/505-7700

1633 Broadway
New York, New York 10019
212/708-1600

MTV NETWORKS
10 Universal City Plaza
Universal City, California 91608
818/505-7800

1515 Broadway
New York, New York 10036
212/258-8000

NBC (National Broadcasting Company)
3000 West Alameda
Burbank, California 91523
818/840-4444

30 Rockefeller Plaza
New York, New York 10020
212/664-4444

NICKELODEON
10 Universal City Plaza
33rd Floor
Universal City, California 91608
818/505-7800

1515 Broadway, 21st Floor
New York, NY 10036
212/258-7500

PBS (Public Broadcasting System)
3171 Los Feliz Boulevard
Suite 203
Los Angeles, California 90039
213/667-3488

1790 Broadway, 16th Floor
New York, New York 10019
212/708-3000

PLAYBOY TELEVISION
9242 Beverly Blvd.
Beverly Hills, California 90210
310/246-4000

SHOWTIME NETWORKS
10 Universal City Plaza
Universal City, California 91608
818/505-7700

1633 Broadway
New York, New York 10019
212/708-1600

TELEMUNDO
2340 West 8th Street
Hialeah, Florida 33010
305/887-6714

TBS (Turner Broadcasting System)
One CNN Center
P.O. Box 105366
Atlanta, Georgia 30348
404/827-1136

UPN (United Paramount Network)
5555 Melrose Avenue
Los Angeles, California 90038
213/956-5000

15 Columbus Circle
New York, New York 10023
212/373-7000

USA NETWORK
2049 Century Park East
Suite 2550
Los Angeles, California 90067
310/277-0199

1230 Avenue of the Americas
New York, New York 10020
212/408-8823

WB (The Warner Bros. Network)
3701 West Oak Street
Building 34R
Burbank, California 91505
818/954-6000

75 Rockefeller Plaza
New York, New York 10019
212/484-8000

MAJOR STUDIOS

MGM (Metro-Goldwyn-Mayer)
2500 Broadway Street
Santa Monica, California 90404
310/449-3000

Paramount Pictures
5555 Melrose Avenue
Los Angeles, California 90038
213/956-5000

15 Columbus Circle
New York, New York 10023
212/373-7000

Sony Studios
(Columbia Studios, Sony Pictures
Entertainment, TriStar Pictures)
10202 West Washington Boulevard
Culver City, California 90232
310/280-8000

550 Madison Avenue, 8th Floor
New York, New York 10022
212/833-8833

20th Century Fox
10201 West Pico Boulevard
Los Angeles, California 90035
310/277-2211

40 West 57th Street
New York, New York 10019
212/977-5500

Universal Studios
(Includes: MCA, Inc.)
100 Universal City Plaza
Universal City, California
818/777-1000

445 Park Avenue
New York, New York 10022
212/759-7500

Walt Disney Studios
500 South Buena Vista Street
Burbank, California 91521
818/560-1000

P.O. Box 10200
Lake Buena Vista, Florida 32830
407/827-5353

Warner Bros. Studios
4000 Warner Boulevard
Burbank, California 91522
818/954-6000

75 Rockefeller Plaza
New York, New York 10019
212/484-8000

GLOSSARY

8 X 10

An actor's photograph, usually in black-and-white, and measuring eight inches in width by 10 inches in height.

ABOVE THE TITLE CREDIT

A billing term that designates that a performer's screen credit shall appear before the title of the film or project. Usually reserved for stars whose names should help draw an audience.

ACTOR LIST

Compiled by a casting director, a list of appropriate non-name-value actors for a particular role in a project.

ADDITIONAL DIALOGUE REQUIRED (ADR)

See Looping.

ADJUSTMENT (Direction)

A directorial note given to an actor during the audition process by a casting director, casting associate, director, producer or writer.

AEA (Actors Equity Association)

Performers' union which enforces, negotiates and assures fair working conditions, salaries and benefits in professional theatre productions.

AEA SIGNATORY

A producer or production company which has signed an agreement which states they shall adhere to the Actors Equity Association's union contract. AEA actors may not work for a non-AEA signatory company without prior permission from the union.

AFTRA (American Federation of Television and Radio Artists)
Performers' union which enforces, negotiates and assures fair working conditions, salaries and benefits in soap operas, television, newscasts, commercials, recordings and radio projects.

AFTRA SIGNATORY
A producer or production company which has signed an agreement which states they shall adhere to the American Federation of Television and Radio Artists' union contract. AFTRA actors may not work for a non-AFTRA signatory company without prior permission from the union.

AGENT
See *Commercial Talent Agency* and *Theatrical Talent Agency*

AGE RANGE
A five-year span of age that an actor feels he or she can realistically portray.

AGVA (American Guild of Variety Artists)
Performers' union which enforces, negotiates and assures fair working conditions, salaries and benefits in areas not covered by SAG, AEA, or AFTRA contracts, including non-broadcast cabaret performances, circuses, and stand-up comedy appearances.

AMERICANS WITH DISABILITIES ACT
Federal law stating that all public buildings must be accessible to the handicapped.

ARTIOS AWARDS
The "Oscars" of the casting world. Awarded by the Casting Society of America, Artios awards are handed out once a year at a banquet to celebrate outstanding achievements in theatrical, feature, and television casting.

ATMOSPHERE
A term given to a group of extra performers working on a project. (*See also: Extras*)

AT PRODUCER'S DISCRETION
A term included in contracts which indicates that a specific detail shall be determined solely by the producer at a later date.

AUDITION
An interview for an acting job at which an actor reads lines of dialogue from a specific script.

AUDITION CRASHING
An unwelcome practice whereby an actor shows up for an audition without an official appointment.

AVAILABILITIES
Process whereby a casting director checks to see if an actor is and interested in a particular role in a project and is not otherwise booked.

BEING IN CHARACTER
Attending an audition as the character without revealing your own personality to the casting director or producers.

BILLING
On-screen credit for an actor or technician.

BLACK-FACING
A practice whereby a non-African American actor is hired to play an African American role. The actor may or may not be made to appear African American through prosthetics or makeup. Seldom used in the entertainment industry. Example: Al Jolson in THE JAZZ SINGER (See also: Brown-Facing; Yellow-Facing.)

BLIND SUBMISSION
When an actor sends a picture and resume to a casting director, agent, manager, director or producer without any prior contact.

BOOKED
Term designating that an actor has been hired.

BREAKDOWN
A brief synopsis of the plot, characters, and production information of any given play, series, episode, movie-of-the-week or feature film which is released by casting directors and distributed to union-franchised talent agencies through Breakdown Services, Inc.

BROWN-FACING
A practice whereby a non-Latino or non-Native American actor is hired to play a Latino or Native American role. The actor may or may not be made to appear Latino or Native American through prosthetics or makeup. A very common practice in the entertainment industry. (See also: Black-Facing; Yellow Facing)

BUMPS
Contractual term referring to raises in salary.

BUSINESS AFFAIRS
Department in a studio, network or independent production company which is dedicated to negotiating detailed contracts for employment.

CALLBACK (Producers' Session)
An audition (often following a preread) at which the casting director, producers, director, and writer are usually present.

CAMEO
A brief appearance (usually by a celebrity) in a television program or feature film.

CARDS
A billing term designating that a performer's on-screen credit shall not roll by in a crawl but appear on screen for a certain amount of time.

CAST CONTINGENT

Term used by executives to indicate that the proposed project shall be approved or financed for production only if an acceptable cast can be found.

CASTING COUCH (Sexual Harassment)

Term given to the practice of a producer, casting director, or other production personnel offering employment or the possibility of employment to an actor in return for sexual favors.

CASTING ASSISTANT (Casting Coordinator)

Individual in a casting office responsible for scheduling, filing, fielding phone calls, and other miscellaneous duties.

CASTING ASSOCIATE

Position between casting assistant and casting director. Depending on the dynamics of the office, a casting associate can do as much as audition actors, give callbacks, negotiate deals, or as little as scheduling, filing, fielding phone calls and other miscellaneous duties.

CASTING DIRECTOR

Individual(s) or company hired by a network, studio or production company to locate, present, and negotiate for the services of on-screen, principal talent.

CASTING INTERN

Individual in a casting office responsible for various duties—from filing to faxing—who provides their services for little or no pay in exchange for experience or college course credit.

CASTING SOCIETY OF AMERICA (C.S.A.)

An organization of professional film, television and theatre casting directors. Membership is earned by acquiring two years of online casting experience, payment of dues, and the recommendation of other current members. The C.S.A. has offices in New York and Los Angeles. Not all casting directors are members of the C.S.A.

CATTLECALL (Open Call)
A large-scale audition where, through trade papers or popular press, all professional and/or amateur actors are encouraged to attend.

CHECK AUTHORIZATION (Check Autho)
A legal form an actor fills out at the request of their agent authorizing production companies to send all actor's paychecks directly to the talent agency office rather than the performer's home. If an agent does not submit a check autho to a casting director once an actor has booked a job, the check will go directly to the actor.

CHEMISTRY READING
An additional step in the audition process where an actor is asked to read with the "star" or another actor so that producers may evaluate the personal interplay between the two actors.

CLOSED
Term indicating that negotiations for an actor's services have been completed, and that all parties are in agreement as to the basic terms of the pending contract.

COLD READING SHOWCASE (Workshop)
A series of ongoing classes taught by a rotation of professional casting directors or associates in which each actor is given or has prepared a scene to read. Actors pay a fee to the showcase organizing company to attend, and casting directors are usually paid a fee for their appearance. These showcases are a popular way for actors to meet casting directors, although participation is not a guarantee of employment.

COMMERCIAL TALENT AGENCY
An individual or company sanctioned by applicable unions to represent union actors exclusively in the field of television commercials. Commercial talent agents submit actors for national and regional television commercials, and negotiate all employment contracts on behalf of their actors. Legitimate commercial talent agencies *do not* charge an upfront fee for representation; however,

they are entitled to ten-percent of any moneys received by clients for whom they have negotiated a deal. Some commercial talent agencies do have theatrical representation departments as well.

COMPOSITE

Incorporating four to five different photographs, a composite is a one-sheet of photographs reproduced on either glossy paper or by means of lithography. Presenting different looks of an actor, composites are primarily used in the television commercial field.

CONTRACT

A legal and binding document containing all employment terms as well as the rights of the employer

CORPORATION (Corp.)

A legal company, licensed by state and federal authorities, formed by working actors who wish to take advantage of the tax breaks afforded to corporations. When hired for a job, an actor who has a corporation must provide the name and federal identification number of the corp which is then paid for the actor's services.

CO-STAR

A role which has a significant amount of screen-time or impact in a project but is not one of the leading roles.

COVER A PROJECT

Term used when a casting director has an associate take control of a project. The casting associate then assumes all casting duties on a project which is overseen by the casting director. Also used by agents when they are assigned to a particular project.

CRAWL

List of names of cast and crew members credited with participation in the making of a television program, mini-series, movie-of-the-week, or feature film. Usually seen on-screen at the end of a project, a crawl (ironicallly) usually goes by at the speed of light. The Screen Actors Guild does supply guidelines as to the length of time a performer's name must appear on the screen, however.

CREDITS
Listing of feature film, television or stage productions in which an actor has appeared or on which a technician has worked.

CUE CARDS
Sheets of posterboard upon which dialogue is written. They are held up, out of camera range, so that a performer may read their dialogue directly from the cards.

DAY PLAYER
A term referring to an actor hired on a daily basis and indicating that the actor has been hired on a daily rather than a weekly contract.

DEAL MEMO
A rough worksheet and brief outline of all deal points negotiated for the services of an artist. Usually never seen by an actor, the deal memo contains information which is transferred to a contract of employment.

DEMO REEL
A series of short clips from an actor's previous screen work which are edited together to give the viewer a sense of the performer's range. Usually no longer that 10 to 12 minutes.

DEVELOPMENT DEAL
An agreement between a producer, production company, studio or network and an artist (actor, writer, producer) to develop a project around that artist's talent. In reference to actors, a development deal is negotiated when executives are impressed with an actor's ability and are willing to commit to creating a project specifically for that actor. Development deals are negotiated by agents and can involve substantial amounts of money as that artist is essentially removed from the market for a period of time.

DIRECTION
See Adjustment.

DIRECTOR
Individual hired for their creative vision and to guide/oversee all aspects of a project's physical production, from casting to editing.

DRAMA
A television, stage, or film project in which character, plot, or relational development is the key to affecting the audience in an emotional way. (e.g., ER, FOREST GUMP, DEATH OF A SALESMAN)

DRESSING ROOM
Facility supplied to artist while on the set or location. Dressing rooms can be private or shared with other actors dependent upon the negotiated contracts.

DRESSING THE PART
Arriving at an audition dressed exactly as the character would dress, regardless of how far from normal street dress. (Example: Sean Young showed up at Warner Bros. dressed as "Catwoman.")

DRESSING APPROPRIATELY
Arriving at an audition dressed in a manner which approximates the dress of a particular character and does not distract the viewer from the reading. (e.g., wearing a suit when auditioning for the role of a lawyer.)

END TITLES
A billing term designating that a performer's screen credit shall appear during the closing credits. It is usually separate from the crawl. In sitcoms, all guest stars, co-stars and featured players appear in the end titles. In hour shows, end titles usually include co-stars and featured players.

EPISODE (EPISODIC) RATE
Contractual point of a test option deal which describes the amount a performer is paid for each episode of a series should it be picked up for broadcast on a network's schedule.

EPISODIC
Term describing television series productions which are broadcast on a weekly basis.

EXECUTIVE CALLBACK (Studio Reading)
An audition for a series regular role at which studio executives are present and must approve of each auditioning actor before that actor tests for network executives.

EXTRA
An individual hired for a production to appear on-camera but without dialogue. There can be union and nonunion extras, and a production company may employ both on the same project

FAVORED NATIONS
Contractual term stating that a certain deal point (e.g., salary, dressing rooms) in an actor's contract shall be equal to all other performers hired to work on the production. If the leads in the project are of significant name-value, favored nations may be applied to all other actors except those leads.

FEATURE FILM
A comedic or dramatic project which is shot on film for exhibition in movie theatres.

FEDERAL I.D. NUMBER
Taxpayer identification number supplied by the Federal Government as an account number for an actor's corporation.

FEEDBACK
An evaluation of an actor's audition given by a casting director to that actor or the actor's agent.

FREE VIDEO CASSETTE
Contractual obligation negotiated by an agent stating that a production will provide an actor or member of the production staff with a standard VHS copy of the finished project when such VHS copies are available.

FULL-BLEED
Term referring to the reproduction of headshots and indicating that the image extends fully to the edges of the photographic paper rather than being surrounded on all sides by white borders.

FULL-SERVICE TALENT AGENCY
An individual or company sanctioned by applicable unions to represent union actors in all areas (theatrical and commercial) of the entertainment industry.

GENERAL INTERVIEW
A meeting between an actor and a casting director, producer or agent at which no audition takes place.

GLOSSY STOCK
See Gloss Tone.

GLOSS TONE
A finish used for actor's headshots, so named for it's nearly-reflective, glossy surface.

GOING TO NETWORK
See Network Test.

GROUP INSTANT-CALLBACK
A producer's audition at which every actor reading is asked to remain in the waiting area until released as one actor will be hired and sent immediately to the set.

GUARANTEED DAYS
The number of days for which a performer is guaranteed to be employed and paid.

GUEST STAR
An actor who is not a series regular but is hired on a weekly contract to play a large role or name-value cameo on an episodic television project.

HEADSHOT
An 8 x 10, black and white photograph of an actor.

HERITAGE-SPECIFIC CASTING
A practice borne of misunderstanding of the term "nontraditional casting," wherein a producer refuses to cast or audition actors who match the ethnicity of the character but are not of the exact specific heritage as the role. (e.g., the only Asian American actors permitted to audition for a Chinese character are Chinese American actors.)

INDUSTRIAL
A film project—filmed under the SAG industrial agreement—which is not produced for theatrical distribution or television broadcast; rather it is produced with the express intent to educate, train or inform individuals on proper procedures or qualities of a project or product.

INSTANT CALLBACK
An audition for the same role which immediately follows or is within a few hours of the initial audition.

INTERACTIVE
Film or videotape project—filmed under the SAG industrial or interactive agreement—which is not produced for theatrical distribution or television broadcast; rather it is produced with the express intent to educate, train, entertain or inform individuals in an interactive format (e.g., video games, theme-park video guides)

LEAD
A role which has significant screen-time or impact in a project.

LITHOGRAPH
An inexpensive alternative to gloss or pearl tone in the reproduction of actor's headshots. Lithographs are photos reproduced in halftones (dots-per-inch) on a lightweight paper.

LOCATION
Term given to the locale of a film shoot day when that day's work is not filmed in a studio or on a sound stage.

LOOPING (ADR)
Rerecording of a project's dialogue after filming has been completed. Usually necessary when noise interferes with onset sound recordaing; to change adult language to milder language for future television broadcast; or to provide additional required dialogue.

LOW BUDGET FEATURE
A feature film with a budget of $2 million or less and produced under the SAG Low Budget Agreement.

MAIN TITLES
The first appearance of any screen credit following the title of the project.

MAJOR ROLE PERFORMER SALARY
See Top-of-Show.

MAKEUP CALL
An actor's first call-time for appearance at the set or location in order to have makeup applied and hair styled.

MANAGER
See Personal Manager.

MERCHANDISING FEE
Contractual fee paid to an actor for any merchandise bearing the artist's likeness and created because of the actor's participation in a project.

MINI-SERIES
Usually a dramatic film project made expressly for television; which exceeds two hours in length; which is not on a network's regular weekly schedule; and is shown over a period of at least two nights.

MOVIE-OF-THE-WEEK (MOW)
A feature-length film made expressly for television broadcast and is not slated to appear regularly on a network schedule, but rather as a special presentation.

NAME-VALUE ACTOR
An actor who, based upon performance of their previous projects, has proven box-office appeal or high recognizability within the public eye.

NAME-VALUE LIST

Compiled by casting directors, a name-value list contains the names of recognizable performers whose presence in the project will ensure significant box office revenues, overseas sales, or ratings.

NETWORK

Company carried by national and regional affiliates or on cable systems which broadcasts a set number of hours of programming per week. Networks may or may not produce original programs.

NETWORK EXECUTIVES

Individuals responsible for overseeing the development, scheduling, and casting of pilots, movies-of-the-week and mini-series for commercial broadcast on national television channels.

NETWORK TEST

Final stage in the audition process for series regular roles on television programs, a network test is a reading before the network executives and will result in an actor being approved for employment or not.

NONCONSECUTIVE LOOPING DAYS (NCL Days)

Negotiated by an agent, the number of days under SAG Schedule F that the producers may use the artist for rerecording of dialogue without incurring additional costs. Producers must work around an actor's schedule and may not use these days all in a row. At least one day must separate each use of an NCL day.

NONTRADITIONAL CASTING

The casting of actors of color, actors with disabilities, and female actors in roles where race, ethnicity, physical ability or gender are not essential to the character's or play's development.

NONTRADITIONAL CASTING PROJECT (NTCP)

A not-for-profit advocacy organization whose purpose is to address and seek solutions to the problems of racism and exclusion in theatre, film and television. The NTCP's goal is that one day actors will be cast solely on the basis of individual talent rather than how they conform to stereotypes.

NONUNION

Term designating that a performer or production is not sanctioned by SAG, AFTRA or AEA.

NO QUOTE

Contractual term usually designating that a performer has worked for less than their quoted rate and that no details of an employment contract will be disseminated to any individual outside of the production.

OFFER ONLY

Casting term stating that an actor will not audition for a particular role but would work on the project pending negotiation of an equitable deal.

ON-AIR

Term designating that an unproduced television pilot has a guarantee from the network to be produced along with multiple episodes.

ONLINE CASTING

Term designating that an individual is/was directly responsible for the principle casting of a particular project.

ON-OR-ABOUT (O/A)

Contractual statement used with weekly players in reference to work start dates. If booked on-or-about and if a contract is delivered to an actor at least seven days prior to the start date, producers are permitted to start an actor either on the specified date or within one day of that date in either direction. (e.g., If booked on-or-about February 10, 1996, the production company may actually start the actor on February 9th, 10th, or 11th.)

OPEN CALL
See Cattlecall.

OPENING, ACT I CREDIT
In one-hour series television, screen credit which follows the tease, the main titles, the first commercial break, and as act one of the show begins.

PAID ADVERTISING (Paid Ads)
The names appearing at the bottom of film posters and ads printed in newspapers. Paid ads must be negotiated into a contract. The name is slightly deceptive in that the artist is not paid for the appearance of their name. Rather, the advertising in which the artist's name appears has been paid for by the production company.

PASSING
Decision of an actor not to audition, or accept employment for a particular project.

PAY OR PLAY
Contractual term referring to an artist's right to be paid for all guaranteed days or weeks of employment whether worked or not insofar as the artist was not responsible for any breach of contract.

PEARL TONE
A quality of finish available for actor's headshots which is more flat in tone than a glossy finish. So named because the surface of the picture, when held at a slight angle, has a pearl-like shimmer to it.

PER DIEM
The amount paid to an actor for each day that they are required to be out of town for work on a project, including travel days. Open to negotiation, this fee is meant to cover any meals or personal expenses and may never fall below the minimum per diem rates set by the union.

PER-EPISODE SALARY
See Episode (Episodic) Rate.

PERSONAL MANAGER

An individual or company who represents actors in all areas and usually works in conjunction with the actor's agent through the submission, negotiation, and scheduling process. Personal managers are not governed by any union rules and may not directly negotiate deals for an actor. Legitimate personal managers do not usually charge actors an upfront fee for representation; however, they are entitled to anywhere from ten to 20 percent (depending upon the agreement between actor and manager) of any moneys their client receives.

PHOTO APPROVAL

The negotiated right of an artist to accept or reject a certain amount of publicity photos of themselves.

PILOT

The first produced episode of a proposed television series from which network executives decide if the series will be placed on the network schedule (*picked up*) and how many additional episodes will be ordered.

PILOT SALARY

The amount paid to an actor for their work as a series regular in a television pilot. Part of a test option deal, a pilot salary is negotiated prior to the actor being hired and is usually significantly higher than a per-episode salary.

PITCH

Process by which an agent notes all of an actor's qualifications in an attempt to have their client met by a casting director or producer. Also may refer to a writer or producer making a verbal presentation of a series or film project to a network or studio.

POINTS

Points refers to percentage points of the producers' profits (gross or net profits) derived from a film or television project. Usually negotiated when the actor is of major star caliber or if actor has accepted a significant reduction in salary.

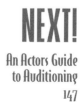

NEXT!
An Actors Guide
to Auditioning
147

POSITION
A negotiable aspect of contractual billing specifying a particular placement of a screen credit in relation to the first screen credit (i.e., first position after the title.)

PREREAD
An audition for a casting director or casting associate only.

PRESENTATION PILOT
A television pilot presented on-stage; one where only a few scenes are put on film; or one produced with considerably less money than a normal pilot.

PRODUCER
Individual within a network, studio or production company who oversees either financial or creative (or both) aspects of a particular film, television or stage production.

PRODUCERS' SESSION
See Callback.

PRODUCTION COMPANY
A company which has developed and produced a film, television or stage production and is responsible for all aspects of physical production, including the payment of actors and technicians.

PRODUCTION NUMBER
An account or code number assigned to a film or episodes of a television project.

PROFIT PARTICIPATION
See Points.

PSYCHING OUT THE COMPETITION
Process by which an actor may consciously or unconsciously attempt to undermine the confidence of other actors auditioning for the same role.

PUBLICIST

Hired by actors, an individual or company responsible for keeping the actor's name and face in the public eye by arranging print and television interviews or personal appearances.

PUT ON TAPE

An actor's audition which is videotaped and shown to the producers and/or director for evaluation purposes.

QUOTE

A brief summation of the major deal points of an actor's last job, series, or network test upon which a casting director or business affairs representative will base their current offer to said actor.

READER

An individual hired (although seldom paid) to read with auditioning actors so that a casting director or associate may give their entire attention to the auditioning actor.

RECURRING CHARACTER

In a television series, a character that is not a series regular but appears in multiple episodes and is usually performed by the same actor for each appearance.

RESUME

A complete list of an actor's film, television, stage and commercial credits, as well as any special abilities, union affiliations, and contact information.

SAG (Screen Actors Guild)

Performers' union which enforces, negotiates and assures fair working conditions, salaries, and benefits in the majority of television projects and commercials as well as all union feature films.

SAG LOW BUDGET AGREEMENT

A Screen Actors Guild contract covering feature films with a total budget of $2 million or less. It allows a lower minimum pay scale than the regular SAG feature contract for use of union actors.

SAG REPORT CATEGORIES

Age, ethnicity, and gender notations on a deal memo which helps actors' unions track hiring statistics in order to address entertainment industry fair hiring practices.

SAG SIGNATORY

A producer or production company which has signed an agreement which states they shall adhere to the Screen Actors Guild's union contract. SAG actors may not work for a non-SAG signatory company without prior permission from the union.

SCALE

Minimum salary payable to a union actor under union rules.

SCALE + 10

Minimum salary payable to a union actor under union rules plus an additional 10 percent as commission for the performer's agent.

SCHEDULE F

Schedule under the SAG agreement which allows a producer to negotiate additional services of an actor without incurring additional costs if the actor's salary is a certain amount or more.

SCREEN TEST

An on-camera audition with full makeup and costumes which is later shown to studio executives and producers. Usually occurs when an actor is considered for a major role in a feature film, although can occur during the casting of a mini-series or movie-of-the-week.

SCRIPT REVISIONS

Color coded pages of a film, television, or stage play which indicate that dialogue or stage directions have changed since the original pages were printed and delivered to actors and production personnel.

SEPARATE CARD
A billing term which indicates that a performer's name shall be the only name to appear on-screen at that particular moment of the credits.

SERIES
A television project which airs once or more per week.

SEXUAL HARASSMENT
See Casting Couch.

SHARED CARD
A billing term indicating that a performer's screen credit shall appear with the names of one or more other performers at the same time.

SHOOT
Term designating the filming of a project.

SHORT FILM
A film project whose entire length is 30 minutes or less.

SIDE-POCKET CLIENT
An actor who has not signed a contract with a union-franchised talent agency but who is unofficially represented and submitted by that agency. Usually occurs when an agent wishes to evaluate their interest in representing an actor, or when an actor has a friend at a large agency who submits them for roles.

SIDES
A set number of pages selected from a script for an actor to read at an audition.

SITUATION COMEDY (Sitcom)
Usually a half-hour television series in which comedy is derived from a set of established characters being placed in different situations each week. (e.g., FRASIER, SEINFELD)

SIZE
Billing term indicating the type size of an individual's on-screen credit in relation to the size of the project's title or other individual's credit.

SKETCH-COMEDY
A television or theatre project in which comedy is derived from a repertory troupe of actors portraying varied characters in a series of different, short scenes. (e.g., SATURDAY NIGHT LIVE, MAD TV)

SPECIAL PROVISIONS
Any special perks or conditions of employment which are not covered in a basic union contract but have been negotiated on an actor's behalf. (e.g., dressing rooms, free looping days, free rehearsal days.)

SPECIAL SKILLS
Section of a resume in which any languages or physical abilities at which the actor is adept are listed.

STACK THE SESSION
Scheduling two to four actor auditions every fifteen minutes in order to keep lapses of time at a minimum in a casting office.

STRAIGHT-TO-PRODUCERS
Term used in casting when an actor reads for the producer and director without prereading for the casting director.

STATION 12
Term indicating that a union actor has not paid all or a portion of his or her union dues and is forbidden to work on a union project until past due funds are paid in full.

STUDIO EXECUTIVES
Individuals responsible for overseeing the development, scheduling, and casting of feature films, video projects, television series, movies-of-the-week and/or mini-series.

STUDIO READING
See Executive Callback.

STUNT CAST

A term indicating that production executives intend to hire an established star for a co-starring or cameo role in order to increase the sales potential of a feature film project or to boost the ratings of a television project.

SUBMISSIONS

Packages containing photographs and resumes sent to casting directors for consideration regarding a certain project.

TABLE READING

The first reading of a script with all cast members present.

TAFT-HARTLEY

Process whereby a non-SAG actor can legally join SAG. If a nonunion actor is hired to work in a SAG project, the casting director or producer must compose a letter to the union which outlines the performer's extraordinary talents which outweigh every other available union actor. If the union grants the "Taft-Hartley," that performer is permitted to work on that project as well as any nonunion projects before joining the guild by payment of dues.

TEST OPTION DEAL (TOD)

A lengthy document used when an actor is in the final stages of consideration for a series regular role on an episodic series or pilot. A TOD is negotiated between an actor's agent and a casting director (or business affairs representative) and includes all the terms of employment for up to five and one-half years. A TOD must be signed by the actor prior to reading at a network test, and should the actor be approved and hired following the test, the TOD automatically becomes the actor's contract.

THEATRICAL TALENT AGENT

An individual or company sanctioned by applicable unions to represent union actors exclusively in the field of stage, television and feature film productions. Theatrical talent agents submit actors for these projects and negotiate all employment contracts on behalf of their actors. Legitimate theatrical talent agencies do not charge an upfront fee for representation; however, they are entitled to ten-percent of any moneys received by clients for whom they have negotiated a deal. Some theatrical talent agencies do have commercial representation departments as well.

THIRTEEN ON-THE-AIR
A television pilot which has received an order from the network for thirteen episodes even before the pilot episode has been produced.

THREE-CAMERA
A screen project that employs three (and sometimes four) cameras while filming. Usually indicates that a show is a sitcom and filmed before a live studio audience.

TOP-OF-SHOW
The minimum salary due and payable under SAG agreements to an actor who is performing a major (guest starring) role in an episodic television program. Top of show, while being a union minimum, is very often the maximum producers will pay for a major role performer who is not of name-value.

TRADES
Magazines and newspapers referred to by entertainment industry members which keep them updated on ratings, production deals, and miscellaneous industry news. (e.g., DAILY VARIETY, THE HOLLYWOOD REPORTER, DRAMA-LOGUE, BACKSTAGE.)

TRAVEL DAYS
As required by the Screen Actors Guild, one day on either side of an actor's work start and work finish days when that actor is required to travel outside of their local area for employment. An actor is paid per diem for each of these days but is not paid a salary unless paid travel days are negotiated.

UNDER 5
An on-camera role which has five or fewer lines of dialogue.

UNION
An organization which oversees fair salaries and working conditions for employees within a specific field.

UNION AFFILIATION
Usually noted on a resume, the unions to which the performer belongs.

UNION FRANCHISED
A talent agency sanctioned by applicable performer's unions and bound by said union's rules and regulations.

VITAL STATISTICS
Section of an actor's resume which includes personal information such as eye-color, height, weight, and age-range.

VOICE-OVER
An acting job where only an actor's voice shall be used in the production.

WARDROBE FEE
Amount an actor shall be paid for providing their own wardrobe for a production. Minimum fees are governed by unions but can be negotiated by an agent.

WEEKLY PLAYER
A term referring to an actor hired for a film or television project for a minimum of five consecutive days.

WORK-STOP DATE
Contractual obligation negotiated by an agent stating that a production will not work an actor past a set date.

YELLOW-FACING
A practice whereby a non-Asian American actor is hired to play an Asian or Asian American role. The actor may or may not be made to appear Asian American through prosthetics or makeup. Very common in the entertainment industry. (See also: Black-Facing and Brown-Facing.)

INDEX

SYMBOLS

5-Day Weekly Contract 94
8-Day Weekly Contract 94

A

Additional Dialogue Required (ADR)
 96
Adjustment/Direction
  30, 32, 73, 74, 75, 76
Age
 Being asked your 77, 78
 Range 15, 78
Agent 1, 3, 5, 8, 11, 16,
  20, 22, 30, 34, 35, 36, 37, 43,
  44, 46, 47, 49, 50, 52, 53, 60,
  64, 67, 68, 72, 76, 77, 78, 80,
  81, 82, 83, 84, 85, 89, 91, 92,
  93, 94, 95, 97, 100, 103, 109,
  112
 Commission 109
 Finding one 111
    Blind submission 112
    Cold-reading showcases 112
 Up-front fees 109
Americans with Disabilities Act 64

Audition viii, 1, 2, 3, 6, 20,
  23, 24, 29, 33, 47, 50, 52, 53,
  54, 57, 58, 59, 61, 63, 64, 65,
  66, 67, 68, 69, 70, 71, 72, 74,
  75, 76, 77, 80, 81, 82, 83, 84,
  85, 86, 105, 112, 113
 Being videotaped 80, 81
 Coming in, in character 65
 Crashing 46
 Getting an audition 43
    Agent/manager submission
      43, 44
    Audition crashing 46
    Self submission 45
 Types of 27
    Callbacks
      5, 29, 30, 31, 32,
      33, 34, 35
    Cattle call / open call 27, 28
    Prereads 5, 29
Audition crashing 46
Availabilities 2, 3, 5

B

Being Replaced 103
Billing 95
   Above-The-Title Credits 95
   Crawl 96
   End-Title Credits 96
   Main-Title Credits 96
   Opening, Act I Credits 96
   Position 96
   Separate Card 95
   Shared Card 95
   Size 96
Breakdown 3, 5, 43, 49, 52
   Agents/Managers 43
   Agents/managers and the 5
   Breakdown Services, Inc. 3
   Information included on 5
   Obtaining a copy 49
Bumps 35

C

Callbacks 29, 30, 31
Casting
   Assistant viii, ix, 3, 24, 29, 36,
      45, 48, 58, 61, 64, 67, 68, 77,
      82, 107
   Associate 3, 24, 25, 29, 48, 114
   Couch 82
   Intern 23
Cattle calls 28
Cigarettes 71
Cold-Reading
   Showcases 113
Common Sense 60
Composite Photograph 9
Conflicting Work Dates 77
Conversation 69, 70
Corporations 91

D

Daily Contract 93
Day-Player 92
Deal Memo 89, 91, 99
Demo Reels 20, 22, 109, 112
   Contact Information on 22
   Editing of 21
   Qualities 20, 21
   Sending to
      Agents/Managers 112
      Casting Directors 22, 107
Dialogue
   Changing 71
Direction/Adjustment
   30, 31, 32, 73, 74
   Asking for 74, 87
   Contradictory Direction
      Receiving 74
   Creative Interpretation 73, 74
   Disagreeing with 75
   Understanding 30, 74
Director
   3, 29, 47, 48, 49, 86, 114
Director of Photography 114
Distraction
   Countering it 72, 73
Dressing the Part 54

E

Ethnic Heritage
   Being asked your 77, 78, 79
      Specific Casting 79
Expenses 98

F

Favored Nations 103
Faxes 107
Federal Taxpayer I.D. 91
Feedback 72, 84, 85
Free Travel Days 93

G

General Interview 45
Guaranteed Days 95

H

Headshot
   7, 16, 27, 43, 44, 60, 106
   Agents/Managers 109, 110
   Casting Directors 14
   Casting directors and your 5
   Commercial vs. Theatrical 9
   Dropping Off
      Casting Directors 108
   Faxing 107
   Mailing of Resume
      Agents/Managers 112
      Casting Directors 106
   Photographers 8
   Qualities of 9, 10
      Agency Logo 11
      Borders 14
      Color vs. Black and White 11
      Glossy vs. Matte 10
      Name Printed on 11
Hotel 99

I

Instant Callbacks 75
   Group Instant Callback 75

L

Listen to what is being said 61
Lists 2, 3, 5
   Actor list 2
   Name-value list 2
Looping (ADR) Days 93, 96, 97
Low-Budget viii, 60, 94

M

Make-Up Call 101
Managers 5, 8, 22, 43, 44, 47,
      60, 67, 85, 100, 109, 110, 112, 113
   Commission 110
   Conference of Personal Managers
      110
   Finding one 112
      Blind Submission 112
      Cold-Reading Showcases 112
      Friend Referral 113
      Industry Referral 114
      Theatre/Film Invitation 113
   Up-Front Fees 110
   What they do 110
Merchandising Fee 35
Mini-Series 28, 29, 33, 34, 91
Movie-of-the-Week (MOW)
      ix, 32, 33, 34, 91, 111

N

Network Executives 2, 35, 49
Network Test 34, 35, 36, 37
   Test Option Deal (TOD) 35, 36, 37
      Deal Points 35
      Your Quote 36
Non-Traditional Casting 78, 79
Non-Traditional Casting Project
      (NTCP) 78, 79
Nudity 81, 82
   Callbacks 81
   Polaroid Cameras 82
   Prereads 81

O

Offensive Material 83
  Accepting an Audition 83
  Passing on an Audition 83
On-or-About 92, 93

P

Parking 63, 64
Pay-or-Play 95
Per Diem 99
Per-Episode Salary 35
Performance Level 101
Phone Calls 107, 108
Physical Interaction with the Casting
  Director 66, 67
Pilot ix, 32, 33, 34, 35, 50
Postcards 105, 106
Prereads 5, 25, 29, 30, 31, 46
Producers 1, 2, 3, 5, 6, 20,
  24, 25, 28, 29, 30, 31, 32, 33,
  34, 35, 36, 37, 46, 50, 52, 63,
  65, 66, 67, 68, 69, 70, 72, 74,
  75, 78, 79, 80, 81, 82, 83, 86,
  93, 94, 98, 101, 102, 108
Producers sessions 5
Props 71
Psyching out the Competition 58
Publicist 109, 111, 112

Q

Quote 36

R

Readers 23, 24
Recurring Characters 94

Resumes 11, 14, 15, 16, 17,
  44, 45, 60, 94, 109
  Agency Logos 17
  Agent/managers and 5
  Agents/Managers 109, 110
  Credit Format 17
  Dropping Off
     To Casting Directors 108
  Mailing of Pictures
     To Casting Directors 106
  Necessary Information 15, 16
  Text Type Style 17
Round Trip Airfare 98

S

SAG
  Low-Budget Agreement 94
  Report Categories 99
Salary 93
  Major Role Performer 94
  Top-of-Show 94
Saying the Wrong Thing 67, 68, 69
Scale 93, 94, 97
  Scale + 10 93
Schedule F 93, 96
Screen Test 34
Script 1, 28, 50, 52, 87, 91, 99
  Bad Scripts 57
  Casting directors and the 2
  First Full Reading 101
  For Other Projects 61
  Managers and the 110
  Not reading the 68
  Obtaining a copy 49
  Returning the 60
  Revisions 99
  Role cut from the 95
  SAG Guidelines 50
Series ix, 3, 29, 31, 32, 34,
  36, 53, 68, 74, 86, 91, 96,
  102, 111

NEXT!

An Actors Guide
to Auditioning

Sexual Harassment 82
Shaking Hands 65, 66
Short film ix
Sides 23, 49, 50, 52, 53, 59, 77
  Faxed 50
  For other characters 61
  Having the wrong sides 77
Sitting or Standing 66
Social Security Number 91
Special Provisions 97
  Dressing Room 97
  Free Video Cassette 97
  Paid Advertising 97
  Profit Participation
      Points 98
  Wardrobe fees 98
  Work stop date 97
Start Date 92
Station 12 99
Straight-to-Producers 68, 69, 74
Studio Executives 33, 48, 49

T

Table Reading 101
Traffic 63

W

Weekly Contract 93
Work Call 99
Work Stop Date 97
Working
  What is expected of you 102
Writer 3, 29, 47, 48, 49, 85,
    86, 108, 114

NEXT!

An Actors Guide
to Auditioning

ABOUT THE AUTHORS

Paul G. Bens, Jr.

Originally from Northern Kentucky, Paul G. Bens, Jr., trained extensively to become an actor, and eventually landed in Hollywood. After two years struggling in Los Angeles, Bens decided that food was more important than fame and, thanks to his casting director, April Webster, made the transition from acting to casting.

As a casting associate, he has worked with many top-notch casting directors and at many of the studios in Hollywood. His credits as an associate include three seasons on the hit NBC series, *Night Court*, as well as numerous television pilots and several feature films.

In 1991, Bens partnered with Pat Melton, also a casting director, to form Melton/Bens Casting. Currently they are casting the new show, *Malcolm and Eddie*, starring Malcolm-Jamal Warner and Eddie Griffin for TriStar and UPN, as well as the second season of the Columbia/TriStar and Fox Network's hit show, *Ned and Stacey*. Melton/Bens handled the original casting for FBC's pilots, *Enemies* and *Between Brothers*. They have also cast *Likely Suspects* (FBC series); *Haunted Lives II* (ABC); a documentary with Whoopi Goldberg entitled, *Rodrigue: A Man and His Dog*; and an all-Asian animated special for ABC entitled, *Po Po and the Magic Pearl*. Melton/Bens has also acted as casting consultants for the Fox Network's reality-based pilots including, *What's So Funny?, Cop Files, The Big Show*, and *Beyond the Call*. Additionally, they have worked on reality-based programs for MTV, Barbour-Langley Productions, FX, and NBC.

A staunch supporter of minority rights, Bens is a Gay American, a strong proponent of equal access for nontraditional casting of minority artists, and co-publisher of the *Asian American Players Guide*.

ABOUT THE AUTHORS

Ellie Kanner, C. S. A.

Born in Bloomfield, CT., Ellie Kanner was introduced to the theatre at Southern Connecticut State University. In 1985 she relocated to Los Angeles to pursue a career in the entertainment industry.

Shortly after arriving, Kanner began her Hollywood career as an assistant at the Irvin Arthur Talent Agency, where she dealt with some of the industry's top stand-up comedians. A year and a half later, she was promoted to head the agency's television and film departments which consisted of . . . her.

Looking for a new challenge, Kanner left the agency in 1989 to take an assistant's position with Champion/Basker Casting where she worked on feature films, movies-of-the-week, pilots, and television series. In 1990, she moved to Lorimar Television, working on *Sisters*, *Homefront*, and the final season of *Dallas*. In her spare time, Kanner also independently cast two features, *High Strung* and *Midnight Heat*.

In 1991, she was promoted by Barbara Miller to Casting Director as Lorimar became Warner Bros. Television, and began working on three pilots: *Have Mercy*, *Just One of the Girls*, and *Time Trax*. Additionally, she cast the 1992-1993 season of *Step by Step*; the 1992-1994 seasons of Time Trax; the pilot and the 1993-1995 season of *Lois & Clark: The New Adventures of Superman*; the pilot and 1994-1995 season of *Friends*, as well as the pilot of *The Drew Carey Show*. She has also cast the independent feature films: *Sleep With Me*; *Kicking & Screaming*; *Quiet Days in Hollywood*; and *Eden*. Recently, she formed her own company, Ellie Kanner Casting and has cast the CBS series, *Courthouse*; FBC's *The Last Frontier*; the television version of Amy Heckerling's *Clueless*; the pilot of ABC's *Sabrina, the Teenage Witch*; the pilot and series of NBC's *Fired Up*, as well as the film, *The Only Thrill* starring Diane Keaton and Sam Shepard.

AND A FEW WORDS
FOR ACTORS . . .

"Don't take the rejections personally. They [the producers and the director] have ideas about the character that you may not be able to fit, regardless of how great a job you do. And relax, above all, RELAX! And, have fun!
—Dean Cain, Actor
Lois & Clark: The New Adventures of Superman

"Actors auditioning for a guest role on a sitcom might want to consider this: The guest character may be a waitress, an executive, a lawyer, a pizza delivery man, but the role is usually the same—to service the series regulars and make them seem even funnier. That's not to say you can't get a few laughs and shine, but your primary purpose for existing in that scene is to further someone else's story."
—David Zuckerman, Writer/Producer
King of the Hill, The Last Frontier, Fresh Prince of Bel Air

"Actors should always come prepared to the audition. There are no excuses. Arrive on time, do the homework by reading the audition material ahead of the time, and know what type of show (broad comedy, serious drama, etc.) the audition is for. This will also sustain a good relationship with a casting director. We want to bring people in who work hard, do their homework, get the job and make us look good.
—Helen Mossler, *Senior Vice President, Talent and Casting,* Paramount Network Television

"When I came to Hollywood from New York City where my background was exclusively professional theatre, I quickly realized that 'knowing' and 'playing' to your realistic type were imperative in order to 'break into' the business of film and television.

"Once you've done that, either through agent representation or exposure to casting directors through reputable workshops, then you can afford the luxury of stretching those perceptions. When you don't book a job it doesn't mean that you weren't worthy or good, just that they went with an actor who interpreted and/or played the role differently."
—Sharon Lawrence, Actress
NYPD Blue

"Nothing compares to holding an audition after going on an audition . . . which is what I do as an actress/producer. Having auditioned thousands of actors there is one thing I'd like to communicate: the people in the room who appear to be sitting in judgment are, in fact, all on your side. We like you already. And, if I'm wrong about that, who cares? Remember Irving Berlin who wrote, "Yesterday they told you you would not go far . . The next day in your dressing room, they hang a star . . . Let's go on with the show."
—Twink Caplan, Actress/Co-Executive Producer
Clueless

BOOKS FOR ACTORS

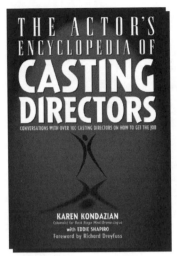

THE ACTOR'S ENCYCLOPEDIA OF CASTING DIRECTORS
Interviews With Over 100 Casting Directors On How To Get The Job
By KAREN KONDAZIAN with EDDIE SHAPIRO
Foreword by RICHARD DREYFUSS

Inside information from premier casting directors in film, television, commercials and theatre from Los Angeles to New York. Casting directors speak on the record to reflect and convey expert advice on how to get in the door and how to prepare effectively for readings. Find out from Casting Directors their personal likes and dislikes, what's hot and what's not, what kinds of pictures and résumés are most successful, common mistakes actors make in auditions, and what directors are looking for.

$19.95

ISBN 1-58065-013-9
original trade paper,
6 x 9, 480 pp.

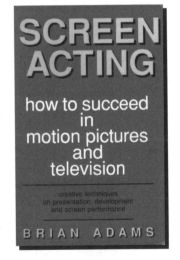

SCREEN ACTING
How to Succeed in Motion Pictures and Television
By BRIAN ADAMS

This comprehensive and practical guide to motion picture and television acting covers personal presentation, acting development and performance techniques for the camera. Fully illustrated, it discusses preparing audition tapes, securing an agent, selecting an acting school, handling screen tests and readings, working with directors, and much more.

$17.95

ISBN 0-943728-20-7
original trade paper
6 x 9, 378 pp.

THE HOLLYWOOD JOB-HUNTER'S SURVIVAL GUIDE
An Insider's Winning Strategies For Getting That (All-Important) First Job...And Keeping It.
By HUGH TAYLOR

Hugh Taylor offers insider's advise on getting that all-important first job, Setting up the Office and Getting to Work, the Script and Story Development Process, Production, Information, Putting it all Together, and Issues and Perspectives.

HUGH TAYLOR received his MBA in business from Harvard's School of Business Administration. He has worked as an assistant to one of Hollywood's top producers moving up from the job of "gofer" to vice president.

$18.95

ISBN 0-943728-51-7
original trade paper
5.25 x 8, 250 pp., illustrated

BOOKS FOR ACTORS

HOW TO GET THE PART . . . WITHOUT FALLING APART!
Featuring the Haber Phrase Technique® for Actors
By MARGIE HABER with BARBARA BABCHICK
Foreword by HEATHER LOCKLEAR

Acting coach Margie Haber has created a revolutionary phrase technique to get actors through readings without stumbling over the script, using a specific, 10-step method for breaking down the scene. Haber's client list includes *Halle Berry, Brad Pitt, Kelly Preston, Heather Locklear, Vince Vaughn, Téa Leoni, Josie Bissett, Vondie Curtis-Hall, Laura Innes, and Tom Arnold*, among others. The book includes script excerpts, celebrity photos, audition stories from today's hottest stars and tips from top industry professionals.

$17.95
ISBN 1-58065-014-7
original trade paper
6 x 9, 360 pp.

MAKING MONEY IN VOICE-OVERS
Winning Strategies to a Successful Career in TV, Commercials, Radio and Animation
By TERRI APPLE, Foreword by GARY OWENS

This book helps the actor, radio DJ, vocal impressionist and amateur cartoon voice succeed in voice-overs, no matter where you live. From assessing one's competitive advantages to creating a demo tape to handling initial sessions, Apple provides a clear guide full of insider tips and strategies helpful to both beginners and experienced professionals.

$16.95
ISBN 1-58065-011-2
original trade paper
5.5 x 8.5, 224 pp.

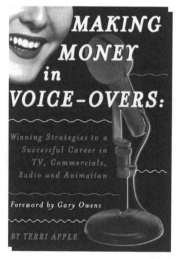

THE GLAM SCAM
By ERIK JOSEPH

Inside THE GLAM SCAM there are psychological profiles of perpetrators, victims and parents, and shocking true stories. THE GLAM SCAM also includes a crash course on who's who in the industry from Acting Coaches, Business Managers, Casting Directors to Producers and Talent Scouts – what they can and can't do for you! Joseph also exposes the most prevalent scams today, state-by-state for all 50 states, as well as Canada. He tells what to look for, and who to call if you suspect a glam scam. If you are working in the entertainment industry, or want to break in, do not go on an audition or answer an ad before reading this book. It could save your life.

$13.95
ISBN 0-943728-66-5
original trade paper
5.25 x 8, 196 pp.

FREE OFFER!

Get a free listing of Hollywood Casting Directors.

We just need your name, street address, city, state and zip code.

1. CALL us toll-free at 1-800-FILMBKS (1-800-345-6257)

2. FAX us at 310-471-4969
   or

3. MAIL a postcard

Our address is:
**Casting Director Offer
Lone Eagle Publishing Co
1024 North Orange Drive
Hollywood, California 90038**